THE SPIRIT
of a
SOUND MIND

SHATINA CHEREE BARR, LMSW

WESTBOW®
PRESS
A DIVISION OF THOMAS NELSON
& ZONDERVAN

Please be advised that you use the suggested strategies in this book at your own risk and it is not recommended that these interventions be used without additional professional consultation, when appropriate.

Unless otherwise noted Scripture taken from the *Amplified Bible*, copyright © 1954, 1958, 1962, 1964, 1965, 1987 by The Lockman Foundation. Used by permission.

Author Credits: LMSW, Evangelist

WestBow Press books may be ordered through booksellers or by contacting:

WestBow Press
A Division of Thomas Nelson & Zondervan
1663 Liberty Drive
Bloomington, IN 47403
www.westbowpress.com
1 (866) 928-1240

Because of the dynamic nature of the Internet, any web addresses or links contained in this book may have changed since publication and may no longer be valid. The views expressed in this work are solely those of the author and do not necessarily reflect the views of the publisher, and the publisher hereby disclaims any responsibility for them.

Any people depicted in stock imagery provided by Thinkstock are models, and such images are being used for illustrative purposes only. Certain stock imagery © Thinkstock.

ISBN: 978-1-4908-7818-8 (sc)
ISBN: 978-1-4908-7819-5 (hc)
ISBN: 978-1-4908-7817-1 (e)

Library of Congress Control Number: 2015906607

Print information available on the last page.

WestBow Press rev. date: 07/13/2015

Contents

Dedication

Firstly, this book is dedicated to my Lord and Savior, Jesus Christ. "For I am not ashamed of the gospel of Jesus Christ: for it is the power of God unto Salvation, to every one that believeth; to the Jew first, and also to the Greek" (Romans 1:16, KJV).

Secondly, to my late maternal grandmother, Pastor Hazel Lee McNair McAlister, who demonstrated to me through her expression of love and commitment to people that God exists. Thirdly, to my mother, Patricia D. Radcliffe, a confidant and supporter as well as my brother, Damone D. Jackson, who I love dearly. Additional thanks to my aunt, Doreen E. McAlister, for the life-long contributions you have made to me personally and professionally as well as your introducing reference material for this book.

Thirdly, to my church family Zion Dominion Global Ministries, under the leadership of Senior Pastor, Roderick L. Hennings and First Lady Pamela D. Hennings. My life will never be the same because of the continued exposure to the preaching and teaching of the Gospel of Jesus Christ through this ministry.

Foreword

It is not often that I read a book or article that challenges me to rethink the psychology of the Christian mind. However, this book by Shatina C. Barr did just that! The mind is inextricably complicated; yet, Ms. Barr has meticulously confronted a web of facts and feelings that construct our mental experiences and provides a sonogram of how to engage, as we imagine and dialogue with things that dictate our destiny. This book is a tool that aids the reader in reevaluating the perspective of what is important and significant not only for Christians but also the secular or academic community, as it relates to embracing a balanced integration between faith and mental health.

It's a matter of mental dominion!

Roderick L. Hennings,
CEO/Sr. Pastor of Zion Dominion Global Ministries
National Director of Church Growth and Development for the Church Of God in Christ, Inc. (COGIC)
White House Liaison for the COGIC
www.ziondominion.org

Acknowledgements

I would like to sincerely thank those who provided their professional guidance and support. Your significant input assisted with the construction and completion of this book.

Dr. Karen Boyd White, Psy.D., Assistant Professor, Department of Psychology, Norfolk State University

Ronjonette Harrison, LCSW-R, Licensed Clinical Social Worker, Transformational Opportunities, Buffalo, New York

Dr. Michael G. MacLean, Ph.D., Department of Psychology, SUNY Buffalo State

Editorial Assistance: Heather Duncan and Jaree Brown Weston

Special Thanks

Crystal D. Jackson, MS; Damenica D. McAlister, MA and Dr. Ernestine A.W. Duncan, Ph.D., Associate Professor, Department Chair of Psychology, Norfolk State University

Introduction/Preface

From sky rocketing ratings in reality shows to an overabundance of reporting personal daily activities on social media sites, it is apparent that society is interested in being exposed to and critiquing human behavior. But, the desire to understand human behavior is not unique to this day and time. Greek philosophers such as Socrates and Plato as well as psychologists like Sigmund Freud and B.F. Skinner and many others in the social sciences have long attempted to define and address psychological functioning. At the same time, medical researchers and doctors such as neurologists and neuroscientists who represent the hard sciences want to help relate or improve human behavior by way of conducting experiments that aim to understand brain functioning in a physical capacity. The list of diverse academic disciplines involved in the study of human behavior could continue, but it is inarguable that we as humans are interested in understanding human life and activity. I too have questions about why people do what they do, but the aim of this book is not to pose a plethora of questions per se, but rather to suggest an additional lens for viewing mental or behavioral health through- the Bible.

Whenever I go to see the optician for an eye exam, he provides several lens options to improve my vision. In an attempt to obtain the perfect fit, several lens combinations are provided. Behavioral or mental health is a complicated matter so using multiple lenses including both faith and science can be beneficial. For instance, a psychiatrist who prescribes medication to stabilize an individual's biochemical processes is using one type of lens for understanding and treating mental health. A primary care physician who informs a patient that he or she should exercise more in order to increase energy levels to combat feelings of sadness can be considered to be using a holistic lens for responding to a behavioral health concern. My argument is that a therapist who uses faith-based interventions to address mental health by incorporating Scripture into therapy should also be considered to be using a valid lens in approaching interventions for treating psychological functioning.

Where Are the Gaps?

At present, there are significant gaps in terms of available material and discussion that is supportive of the interplay between faith, mental health theory and interventions. Frequently, when there is a gap between human understanding and postulation, there inevitably are flaws derived in the theoretical output and subsequent interventions developed. Specifically, such gaps can be found in the educational curriculum. That is to say, post-secondary education students in many colleges and universities are not exposed to the connection between mental health and the Bible. Pupils are not necessarily educated on the origins of mental health from a biblical perspective, or when faith is referenced in class, students are advised that the Bible is a mythical document that cannot be taken literally. From my perspective, clinical students who become mental health practitioners would gain a broader respect for the integration of theology and clinical theory, if and when such gaps are closed. Not surprisingly, the gap in the literature grows larger when seeking information regarding evidence- based interventions and faith in practice. Anti-faith influences on the social sciences hinder a successful collaboration between faith and clinical practice. Some of these hindrances are intricately woven into the fabric of clinical theory.

For the purpose of understanding the basis and argument of this book, it will be important to address three critical assumptions 1) The God of the Bible exists, 2) From a creationist perspective, God created all things including the human mind and 3) The words of the Bible have been given by God to humans in order to understand the world and ourselves and in many instances require a literal application, as opposed to a metaphorical one. Keeping these three points in mind as you read this book is critical in aiding your acceptance of my position, because if you the reader do not understand why I make such matter of fact conclusions in this book, there could be ambiguity on my claims.

The fundamental assumption of this book is that since God created everything, including the mind, there are relevant instructions for addressing mental health phenomena in the Bible. Therefore, we will explore how to understand some underlying root issues of mental health and how to use biblical methods for addressing behavioral health problems. I caution readers who at first glance may presume that I am suggesting that mental health treatment should revert back to an uneducated and uninformed approach that rejects science. However, this is not my position. Rather, I am suggesting a truly holistic approach to treating mental health that does not underestimate the efficacy of faith in practice; simply because the clinician or therapist is under-prepared to address this matter.

Potential Benefits of Including Faith in Practice

The intent of this book is to offer a proposal on how to close the gaps between Christian theology and clinical practice. I will argue for the need for an increase in literature and clinical interventions that promote and speak to the faith of the client actively being used in treatment, when appropriate, to help reach his or her clinical goals. As previously mentioned, if psychology and other mental health curriculums are redesigned in a manner that allow coursework to address Christian theology as valid in treating mental health, graduates would have tools that speak to and support their patients. With more people seeking help for mental health issues it is crucial that clinicians be better equipped to assist those who are suffering with mental illness, particularly those clients who practice their faith and are not willing to abandon its influence upon entering the therapy room. While a faith-based approach is sought for treating illness in general the usage increases especially when the illness is psychiatric and there are high uncertainties regarding the perception of causation and prognosis (Kar 2008, 729).

The integration of faith with clinical practice not only promotes cultural competence, but also offers a holistic approach to treating mental health. Religion has always been a powerful force in human history; yet, in the field of psychology individuals that become familiar with or endorse religious faith are sometimes negatively branded. Researchers and clinicians need not view this integration as regression but rather progression. To this end, my main agenda is to show that there is a valid need for the clinical field to acknowledge and integrate a framework from a biblical perspective as it relates to the assessment, application and development of interventions in dealing with mental health. Therefore, this book will provide a biblical response to understanding and addressing mental health.

CHAPTER 1

The Perfect Fit

Since I was a young girl, I knew I wanted to listen to people and give them advice. Sometimes, while playing kickball with friends, I would imagine providing counseling services as a clinician. Understanding human behavior was a part of my dream. The mystery of the mind is not mine alone, however, as was stated in the preface. The apostle Paul, for instance, was essentially examining his own behavior when he submitted the following statement in a letter to the church in Rome:

"For I do not understand my own actions [I am baffled, bewildered]. I do not practice or accomplish what I wish, but I do the very thing that I loathe [which my moral instinct condemns]" (Rom. 7:15).

I guess at some point and time in life, cognitive reasoning compels us to try to understand not only other people's behavior but our own as well. While studying the mind was and is part of my aspiration, so is studying the Bible. Living as a Christian, studying the Bible and striving to apply its principles are the overwhelming desires of my heart. Therefore, it is the perfect fit for me to integrate both areas into my development and contribution to the world in formulating this book. Although I may digress, the overall point I am making in the next section is that faith and education have not typically been presented as compatible.

Faith and Education

When I began to actualize my dream by attending college, I realized that some students were not as sure of what they wanted to accomplish in school as I was. Many students meandered through the college curriculum, taking elective courses to explore a variety of fields as possible majors. For some, this was plausible, and they discovered their passion, while for others it became a distracting process to not commit to any domain of education. The uncommitted group inevitably found themselves half-way through college without having declared a major. However, this was not the case for me. Upon entering college, I knew which major I would apply to: psychology.

I can remember being disappointed in undergraduate school when I was informed I had to take prerequisite courses, before I could be accepted as a psychology major. Nonetheless, I stayed my course because I knew my deepest academic passion was to study the mind.

I would like to discuss two other courses that had a significant impact on me- philosophy and anthropology. While I enjoyed these classes, I vividly recall instances when I was offended and spoke out during lectures. In the anthropology class, I was not offended by the purported facts regarding where scientists had discovered artifacts or how past civilizations lived. In philosophy, it was not the explanation of how the Socratic method was used in discourse that disturbed me. Rather, my objection in both classes was with the presentation of the information, as opposed to the content thereof. For example, some professors chose to use the lecture hall not only to perform their collegiate responsibilities but also as a platform to discredit the existence of God. My hope of finding the perfect balance between science and God was shattered, as certain professors bullied students into choosing a perspective to support, which, in the end, was science over God.

Later, when I was accepted into my major and began taking psychology classes, the anti-God theme continued in varying degrees. I recall being in an introductory psychology class with hundreds of other students, and the professor described a hideous murder that had occurred. He indicated that he and the several other psychologists who were making an assessment of the alleged murderer were not people who believed in God, necessarily, but the conclusion they derived was that the killer's behavior was driven by an evil force. It was and is interesting to me that for some, the awareness of evil can exist in their thinking independent of an acknowledgment of God, when you actually need one to define the other. It is a sensible dichotomy because if there is up, there is down; if there is left, there is right, and for evil (the Devil), there is good (God), as logic does not allow you to define one without the other. Undergraduate school was the beginning of my awareness and exposure to the blatant disregard for God in academic settings, but it did not stop there.

When I was in training as a clinician in graduate school, there was little to no material available regarding how students could prepare to address faith in practice. The closest I came to this concept was with spirituality in social work. But spirituality is not the same as faith. When the dimensions of spirituality and religion are conflated, misinterpretations and inaccuracies can develop (Del Rio and White 2012, 125). While it is commendable for social work to acknowledge spirituality, I, too, affirm an operational difference between spirituality and faith in God. One can be spiritual and not place his or her faith in God. So then, what is faith, and what would it look like in clinical practice? I will use a biblical definition of faith:

> "For we have heard of your faith in Christ Jesus [the leaning of your entire human personality on Him in absolute trust and confidence in His power, wisdom, and goodness]"(Col. 1:4).

As is indicated by the seriousness of this scriptural definition, faith, when it is genuine, is not something that the possessor can easily or would ever dismiss. For this reason, when a clinician comes in contact with a person of Christian faith in a clinical setting, he or she should be prepared to address this subject with a certain level of familiarity and comfort. From a cultural competency perspective, students should have access to training in faith-based theory. However, we students at that time could not have access to what did not exist. The integration and application of faith are essential in various forms of therapeutic assessments, which should be included in clinical education and intervention development.

Some research shows that only 13 percent of doctoral training programs in North America offer a course in religion or spirituality (Masters 2010, 399). Clearly, there are not enough educational opportunities to adequately prepare students to deal with the potential spectrum of faith-based needs they will face in clinical settings. However, without adequate training, clinicians generally have a decreased comfort level with engaging the client on this subject matter. In addition, a perceived lack of understanding regarding the relevance of faith in practice from the therapist can hinder the therapeutic process for the client.

Faith and Clinical Practice

A practical example of how faith and mental health can meaningfully coincide is with lethality and suicide assessment. The purpose of the lethality assessment is for the clinician to determine what level of risk the client presents with regard to taking his or her own life or someone else's, and the safety plan is a document constructed by the therapist and client that identifies what steps the client can take to prevent suicidal or homicidal behaviors and gestures. These steps could range from attending religious services and talking with their pastor, to contacting suicide prevention agencies. In clinical practice, some lethality assessments recognize the importance of faith by asking the client if he or she has faith-based supports that can be integrated into the safety plan. Such questions attempt to assess the meaningfulness of faith to the client in times of crisis by asking the client if he or she identifies with a particular religion, and if so, if he or she attends religious service and if they are beneficial.

If it is deemed useful and necessary for safety coordination to incorporate the client's Christian faith into aspects of suicide and risk prevention, it is even more important to integrate faith-based interventions into clinical training. When receiving a formal education, clinicians should be made aware of the intimate connection between faith and successful treatment. If the clinician does not understand the value of faith in practice, there may well be a significant oversight in this area in client care. For instance, a clinician who has been trained in faith-based training and interventions could reference the following Scripture with a Christian client who is suicidal:

> "He who is loose and slack in his work is brother to him
> who is a destroyer and he who does not use his endeavors

to heal himself is brother to him who commits suicide"
(Prov.18:9).

Referencing this Scripture in safety planning could accomplish three things: show the client that the therapist has an understanding of his or her faith; remind the client that suicide is not God's will for mankind, and allow the client to discuss his or her feelings surrounding faith and depression in a therapeutic setting.

Safety Planning and Faith
Within the Penal System

As a disclaimer, this section was written in collaboration with a psychologist, who chose to be anonymous:

Can integrating a Christian worldview be addressed with prisoners and/or offenders? More specifically, can talking about an individual's relationship with God be effective in coping with suicidal ideation while incarcerated? According to a consultant psychologist working in the penal system, it appears that a number of offenders find renewing their relationship with God has been effective in helping them cope with their incarceration and heal from significant mental health distress. Consider a testimonial of such an inmate.

"During a conversation with an inmate who was placed on suicide watch, he explained his contemplation of death, as he considered his past lifestyle. He reported that crimes he committed over 27 years ago, left him homeless, hooked on drugs, and living a back-and-forth pattern of incarceration and now that he was in jail, he could see no purpose for living as his life was not significant even when out of jail. However, when faith and God were interjected in the conversation, this inmate began to express a sense of hope. Thusly, he agreed to contract for safety. This spiritually reclaimed prisoner then set goals for himself and was very optimistic about his future and expressed a desire to assist others upon his release."

Needless to say, it cannot necessarily be extrapolated from this testimonial that all offenders will be "saved" and/or have a change of heart and experience a decrease in suicidal thoughts and/or behaviors upon God being referenced in conversation. However, some prison personnel have reported that a vast majority of offenders accept Bibles and do discuss how reading thereof empowers them to cope with their incarceration and overall mental health.

With the overcrowding of prisons and mental health facilities, it is clear that a new direction is needed in treating mental health. With this perspective, high recidivism rates could be an indication that people are not undergoing the type of change in their thinking that leads to sustained improvement. I propose that more advocacy be done on the state and ultimately the federal level concerning the potential value of faith-based interventions when treating mental health in the penal system also.

The Bible and Suicide

The Bible provides a picture of both sides of the coin regarding suicide, as it not only reflects God's displeasure with suicide but also gives a record of individuals who, although they believed in God, when overwhelmed did request of God to die. Two such men, Jonah and Elijah, were both prophets of God, but found themselves asking God to kill them because they felt overwhelmed (1 Kings 19:4; Jonah 4:9, author's paraphrase).

Job is another biblical man (who we will discuss more in the next chapter) who when overcome with grief questioned and wished he had not been born.

> "Why then did You bring me forth out of the womb? Would that I had perished and no eye had seen me! I should have been as though I had not existed; I should have been carried from the womb to the grave" (Job 10:18-19).

Using the example of these men in therapy could connect the client with his or her faith in the most powerful way by helping them realize that although it is not God's instruction for us as humans to take our own lives, it can be a part of the human experience to have suicidal thoughts. Jesus Christ Himself, when dealing with the knowledge of His impending crucifixion, was so overcome with emotion that He could have died from the stress alone.

> "...Jesus told his disciples, "sit here while I pray." He took Peter, James, and John with him. He plunged into a sinkhole of dreadful agony. He told them, "I feel bad enough right now to die..." (Mark 14:32-34, MSG, author's paraphrase).

The clinician who familiarizes him or herself with these type of relevant supportive Scriptures can potentially help patients understand that they are not alone in their hopeless feelings, and this awareness could possibly remove feelings of isolation and shame that result from the feelings of suicide. Frequently, when people are suicidal, there is a sense of hopelessness and perhaps an inability to feel comforted that leads to the view that death is the only way to escape the pain. In an attempt to further comfort the patient, the therapist could also reference the next piece of Scripture:

> "Blessed be the God and Father of our Lord Jesus Christ, the Father of sympathy (pity and mercy) and the God [Who is the Source] of every comfort (consolation and encouragement), Who comforts (consoles and encourages) us in every trouble (calamity and affliction), so that we may also be able to comfort (console and encourage) those who are in any kind of trouble or distress, with the comfort (consolation and encouragement) with which we ourselves are comforted (consoled and encouraged) by God" (2nd Cor. 1:3-4).

Cultural Competence in Practice

The concept of cultural competency can suggest the provider has a level of proficiency regarding relevant cultural variables of the client's treatment. Of course, clinicians can and should independently seek opportunities to educate themselves on various cultural issues; however, the greater burden should be borne by the educational systems to provide adequate occasions for learning on such poignant issues of faith and practice.

From my cultural and professional experience, for many people of faith, obtaining a therapist to provide mental health services is taboo. Although more information is needed regarding what percentage of the self-identified Christians have diagnosable mental illness or are active in clinical treatment, I still believe that more training and education regarding faith and mental health is needed at the undergraduate and graduate level. Faith is a critical and important aspect of many people's lives, which they often do not leave outside the therapy session. In fact, if allegiance to one's faith is strong, it can actually deter individuals from seeking secular treatment; therefore, when clients of faith do overcome difficult barriers to engage in therapy, they deserve a clinician who is well-versed in such cultural matters.

A Personal Experience with
Faith and Mental Health:

As a Christian and practicing mental health therapist, I recall instances where addressing matters of faith arose in session. In one such case, I was providing therapy to a young girl who had allegedly been sexually abused. Due to the nature and complexities of the case, I had two administrators supervising me. During a certain session, a family member who was active in the child's treatment attended a family session and appeared to be practicing her faith by speaking in a tongue. Since I am familiar with the biblical practice of speaking in tongues, I was accustomed to that type of manifestation. My exposure to the manifestation of speaking in tongues as well as my professional training regarding signs of mental illness allowed me to direct the family's attention to where the intervention was most needed, which was with the caretaker and not the child. Furthermore, upon assessment of the child, there was no evidence of sexual abuse. In fact, I confronted the caretaker about her behavior as well as the lack of evidence that her granddaughter had been sexually abused. The maternal grandmother then acknowledged that she had resentment towards the father of her grandchild because she believed that the father had wronged her daughter, the child's mother. At that point, it became apparent that this grandmother had psychological issues and was using her granddaughter's account of alleged sexual abuse to incriminate the child's father. After a few sessions with myself and other clinical opinions, I closed the case as there was no conclusive basis to provide treatment on.

Because I believe and accept the gifts of the Holy Spirit to be real, I would not negatively label someone who spoke in tongues as hallucinating, nor would I underestimate someone who claimed that God spoke to them if their described experience was biblically sound; meaning it was not incongruent with what the Bible states. However, this caretaker's expression was not biblically sound (see 1 Corinthians 14:27). Yet, with the current training clinicians receive, it would be a challenge for him or her to not vilify a Christian client who stated that God spoke to them or manifested speaking in tongues. The undermining teachings from many scholarly communities towards expression of the Holy Spirit can perpetuate soft implications that Christian experiences are a form of pseudo-reality and have little to no place in clinical practice.

It took great skill and a comfort level with faith and clinical theory to sift through the complexities of this case. My hope is that other clinicians will be able to receive training that equips them to handle similar cases that they too may face. I use this example to underscore the benefits of clinicians having background knowledge of the Bible.

CHAPTER 2

Why God? Why the Christian Bible?

The events recorded in the Bible of past successes and failures are for our benefit to learn from (Rom. 15:4, author's paraphrase). Inspired by God, men wrote the message of the Bible for mankind to understand and follow.

> "All scripture is given by inspiration of God, and is profitable for doctrine, for reproof, for correction, for instruction in righteousness: That the man of God may be perfect, thoroughly furnished unto all good works" (2nd Tim. 3:16, KJV).

Like a stenographer in a courtroom or a secretary taking minutes capturing every spoken word of the orator, writers such as Moses and the apostle Paul wrote down dictation from God. God gave these men the message that was to be written. Some would argue that in the translation from the original language to King James English, errors have occurred that call into question the integrity of Scripture. Nevertheless, there is significant evidence to support the Bible as an overall valid reference.

Consider how historical documents such as the Nash Papyrus and the Dead Sea Scrolls support ancient biblical writings, as they support the legitimacy of the Bible. Additional validation for the historical accuracy of the Bible arises from the fact that it mentions various ancient cultures and groups such as the Sabeans:

> "And the Sabeans swooped down upon them and took away [the animals]. Indeed, they have slain the servants with the edge of the sword, and I alone have escaped to tell you" (Job 1:15).

The above reference is a biblical account of a robbery and murder related to Job and his suffering and is quoted by an eye-witness messenger. Job's hardship was a well-known crisis during its time, as can be seen from this quote: "then there came to him all his brothers and sisters and all who had known him before…" (Job 42:11, author's paraphrase). The Sabeans were an ancient people who resided in what is currently known as Yemen, in the southwest of the Arabian Peninsula. These groups of individuals were involved in lucrative trading during their existence. The Bible described Job as a wealthy man and a man of substance; therefore, it makes sense that the Sabeans would have viewed him as a target to rob, since they would have likely incorporated the stolen merchandise into their trading business. The fact that the Bible references the Sabeans is a critical point, as it allows us to see that the Bible not only discusses theological information but also relevant cultural and historical events.

Thus far, you may be in agreement with my proposal on further collaboration between clinical theory and biblical scholarship, but wonder why so much emphasis is placed on one particular faith.

According to Scripture, the God of the Bible is the one and only true and living God, based on the following:

> "Hear, O Israel: the Lord our God is one Lord [the only Lord]" (Deut. 6:4).

> "Thus says the Lord, the King of Israel and Redeemer, the Lord of hosts: I am the First and I am the Last; besides Me there is no God. Who is like Me? Let Him [stand and] proclaim it, declare it, and set [his proofs] in order before Me, since I made and established the people of antiquity. [Who has announced from of old] the things that are coming? Then let them declare of future things…is there a God besides Me? There is no [other] Rock; I know not any" (Isa. 44:6-8, author's paraphrase).

> "For when God made [His] promise to Abraham, He swore by Himself, since He had no one greater by whom to swear"(Heb. 6:13).

Based on the exclusivity of only one God, as indicated in these Scriptures, I therefore yield to that position. Certainly many will say "I do not acknowledge or worship the God of the Bible, because I worship another god." As stated in both of these Scripture references, there is only one true God and besides the God of the Bible there is no one greater. This explains why I am using the Christian God as the supreme source of authority. While I do believe that the God of the Christian Bible is the one and only true God, it is appropriate for a clinical therapist to be familiar with critical aspects of the respective faith of his or her clients. But, for the purpose of this book, the emphasis rests on the God of the Bible.

A Personal Experience with
Faith and Mental Health:

Being able to take a definitive stand on relevant issues is at times necessary. I use now a situation in a philosophy course for a more in-depth example of how the professor incessantly made negative comments about God, faith in God and Christians and how my stance encouraged other students. His personal opinion of God and his lack of respect for those who believed in God had nothing to do with the education I or any other student was to receive in his class, but he continued his ranting week after week. I remember sitting in the front row during one such lecture when the professor was mocking God. At that point, I had had enough of his theological tyranny, so I raised my hand to make a comment. He humored me by allowing me to express my disapproval of his verbal conduct. He concluded the conversation by noting that out of all the Christians he had debated with previously, I was the only one who had expressed herself intellectually and not emotionally. After that class, two students approached my desk and offered their support. They confessed that they were Christians as well and admired my courage to speak up which they lacked.

If I had not represented my faith by speaking out appropriately in the classroom, perhaps the peers who approached me later would have continued to suffer silently for the rest of the semester. While I do not know if these same peers would ever model my example in the future, as we did not keep in contact, I do know, at that time, it was a great value for me to specifically advocate for the Christian faith.

CHAPTER 3

What Is Mental Health?

If you have ever considered leasing or purchasing property, you probably have gone through what is called a "walk-through." During this process, the inspector points out the repairs that are needed based on state regulations and/or other requirements. In some states, financing cannot occur until the recommended home improvements from the inspector have taken place.

I liken the walk-through of the home inspection process to some forms of mental illness, because much like damaged parts of a building, our unhealthy thinking needs to be improved. When dealing with the mind, however, the Bible serves as the code of regulations to replace faulty thoughts. In many instances, I believe unaddressed, diseased thoughts can and do lead to various forms of mental illness. But what is mental illness?

Some clergy have defined mental illnesses as continuum disorders which range from mild disorders such as depression to more extreme ones such as psychosis (Leavey et al. 2007, 552). When diagnosing a mental illness, clinicians use various criteria to assess the onset of the condition such as identifying when the symptoms started and so forth. Clients can find it challenging to provide the therapist with an accurate timeframe of when the symptoms began. I think this ambiguity occurs because we can live with dysfunction for long periods of time by making adjustments to compensate. I can remember talking with a family friend before she died of cancer. During a conversation, I asked her when her stomach pain began and she replied by saying "The doctors asked me the same question but it has been going on for so long, I forgot when it started." In the end, this friend went to the hospital when the pain was too much to bear but by that time the cancer was practically untreatable. Like the body, our minds give us signs when there is abnormal functioning, but the question is, are we listening? Often times, we live in such a way that we are not in tune with ourselves or introspective and thus ignore warning signs.

In psychology, the term introspection means that an individual examines or is in observance of their own mental and emotional processes. In other words, if an individual is introspective he or she will judge his or her own thoughts and feelings. Even Jesus Himself demonstrated His inner connection. Christ was so in tune with Himself that He knew when power was exiting from Him.

> "And Jesus, recognizing in Himself that the power
> proceeding from Him had gone forth, turned around
> immediately in the crowd and said, Who touched My
> clothes?" (Mk. 5:30).

When we are not introspective, we fail to assess our own state of mind, or when we do attempt to assess mental functioning, we use the wrong reference against which to examine our thoughts. In either case, both choices can be detrimental to our psychological development and well-being.

When Did Mental Illness Begin?

Scripture provides a basis on which to build in order to gain an understanding of proper mental health. Quite possibly, if people examined themselves more consistently with the word of God, there would be fewer opportunities for unhealthy thoughts to enter our minds and subsequently less development of mental health issues.

Let us examine mental health from a biblical perspective using the first couple, Adam and Eve. In the book of Genesis, God set a limitation for His precious creation, Adam and Eve; they were unable to eat from the tree of knowledge of "good and evil."

> "And the Lord God commanded the man, saying, You may freely eat of every tree of the garden; but of the tree of the knowledge of good and evil and blessing and calamity you shall not eat, for in the day that you eat of it you shall surely die" (Gen. 2:16-17).

While you might have been aware of the sin of disobedience Adam and Eve committed when they ate the fruit from the tree, you may not have necessarily viewed the outcome of their disobedience from a mental health perspective. I propose that Adam and Eve's actions introduced mental illness to humanity, as there were no recorded mental health issues prior to their disobedience.

> "And the man and his wife were both naked and were not embarrassed or ashamed in each other's presence" (Gen. 2:25).

In fact, not only were there no mental health issues, there were literally no problems in Adam and Eve's relationship. "And God saw everything that He had made, and behold, it was very good (suitable, pleasant) and He approved it completely" (Gen. 1:31, author's paraphrase). Later in the chapter, Satan, in the form of a serpent, tempts Eve into eating from the tree of knowledge of good and evil:

> "Now the serpent was more subtle and crafty than any living creature of the field which the Lord God had made. And he [Satan] said to the woman, Can it really be that God has said, You shall not eat from every tree of the garden? But the serpent said to the woman, You shall not surely die, For God knows that in the day you eat of it your eyes will be opened, and you will be like God, knowing the difference between good and evil and blessing and calamity" (Genesis 3:1,4-5).

Unfortunately, Adam and Eve did go against what God asked by eating from the tree that they were not supposed to eat from.

> "And when the woman saw that the tree was good (suitable, pleasant) for food and that it was delightful to look at, and a tree to be desired in order to make one wise, she took of its fruit and ate; and she gave some also to her husband, and he ate" (Gen. 3:6).

I do not believe that it was the knowledge of "good" that God wanted to prevent His children from experiencing, because, again, up to that point everything He had created was good. Rather, it was the knowledge or acquaintance with evil that God was trying to prevent Adam and Eve from being exposed to, due to the delicacy of the mind. So in actuality, the first recorded rule in the Bible is related to the protection of our mental health. Apparently, God knew what the human inhabitants of the garden did not which is that evil knowledge is an inconspicuous path that leads to impaired mental health. God wanted to circumvent Adam and his wife from experiencing what only He alone was capable of handling, which was the awareness of sin.

After Adam and Eve ate from the tree of knowledge of good and evil, they felt guilt which led to accompanying dysfunctional behaviors.

> "Then the eyes of them both were opened, and they knew that they were naked; and they sewed fig leaves together and made themselves apronlike girdles. And they heard the sound of the Lord God walking in the garden in the cool of the day, and Adam and his wife hid themselves from the presence of the Lord God among the trees of the garden. But the Lord God called to Adam and said to him, Where are you? He said, I heard the sound of You [walking] in the garden, and I was afraid because I was naked; and I hid myself" (Gen. 3:7-10).

When a therapist is assessing for mental health illness, much of the criteria rests on how debilitating the condition is and/or the extent to which it impairs the person's day-to-day functioning. This is to say, an individual adult or child, having significant problems performing the expected life functions (e.g., concentrating in school, ability to execute work related duties properly) could be developing or have an undiagnosed mental illness. An undiagnosed person with mental illness may not ever meet with a clinician to receive a diagnosis or treatment, yet "suffer silently" with mental health impairment. Again, I am proposing that the biblical account of Adam and Eve is the first case of behavior dysfunction and mental illness, as their activities of daily living were impacted; they were distressed and had relational problems.

1). Adam and Eve were no longer able to perform their assigned duties, as they were preoccupied with trying to make their fig garments.
2). The guilt they felt impacted their ability to relate to one another; they began blaming each other.
3). Their fear caused them to isolate themselves.

Satan tempted Eve and ultimately deceived her into believing that she could be like God (e.g., have knowledge and power equal to His), then enticed her to eat the fruit. However, what Eve failed to realize was that although she and Adam had the capability to eat the fruit, neither she nor Adam had the mental capacity to handle sin.

> "And the Lord God said, Behold, the man has become like one of Us [the Father, Son, and Holy Spirit], to know [how to distinguish between] good and evil and blessing and calamity" (Gen. 3:22).

This Scripture makes it clear that God was the only one able to handle being exposed to good and evil. Adam and Eve's once pure minds now had to try to handle negative emotions such as guilt and shame regarding their disobedience. Adam and Eve tried to lessen their mental anguish using their own skills. Completely deluded in the belief that their mental torment rested exclusively in the fact that they were naked, Adam and Eve began sewing fig leaves together to make an apronlike girdle. This couple was ignorant to the fact that their nakedness in and of itself was not the issue tormenting them. In actuality, through their disobedience to God's word, sin had entered their minds and nature and they began to experience the torment of their choice. If the problem was simply their nakedness, the fig garbs would have been effective; however, Adam and Eve did not have ability to provide a remedy for their mental plague. Separate from the intervention of God, there was nothing Adam and Eve could do to correct the anguish they felt.

In an act of compassion meant to soothe their now dark reality of the awareness of sin, God provided the first garments ever for Adam and Eve to wear, after the disobedience was addressed.

"For Adam also and for his wife the Lord God made long coats (tunics) of skins and clothed them" (Gen. 3:21).

After their enlightenment, Adam and Eve were unable to maintain their lifestyle in the garden without torment until God dealt with the sin and provided them with a covering. The recognition of sin is troublesome. Additionally, we see the impact of this awareness within the life of apostle Paul as he pointed out exposure to his sin via observation of the Mosaic Law.

> "…if it had not been for the Law, I should not have recognized sin or had known its meaning. [For instance] I would not have known about covetousness [would have had no consciousness of sin or sense of guilt] if the law had not [repeatedly] said, you shall not covet and have an evil desire [for one thing and another]" (Rom. 7:7, author's paraphrase).

In this reference, Paul is acknowledging that his mental anguish or mental health issues developed after he became aware of sin. I use Paul as an example, because like Adam and Eve, he felt an overwhelming sense of guilt when made aware of his transgression. Therefore like Paul, Adam and Eve were experiencing the effects of sin in their minds. Please note, there are a variety of instances when people may suffer with mental health issues not because of their choices but rather because of someone else's, such as those who have been victims of sexual abuse. However, for the purpose of this section, I am focusing on the impact that comes as a result of our own choices.

Staying Within the Boundaries

When the effects of sin begin to tear the human mind apart, there is healing available and it ultimately has to come from God.

> "So repent (change your mind and purpose); turn around and return [to God], that your sins may be erased (blotted out, wiped clean), that times of refreshing (of recovering from the effects of heat, of reviving with fresh air) may come from the presence of the Lord... "(Acts 3:19).

God's original plan and purpose was not for Adam, Eve, Paul, nor you and I to experience the incapacitating effects that sin has on the mind. Some actions of sin we may commit today could be anything from harboring unforgiveness to practicing deceit and lying. Nonetheless, the effects of sin do continue to plague humanity to this day, as immoral choices and actions do carry a negative impact by way of suffering in one's own body and personality (Rom. 1:27, author's paraphrase).

Adam and Eve's mental health were protected as long as they were obedient. Unrestrained exposure to sin has devastating effects on the mind, much like a computer that has been taken over by a destructive virus. All of the computers I purchased have been equipped with at least a trial version of anti-virus software. In this day and age, it is technological suicide to have a computer with an insufficient defense system. With the prevalence of hackers and viruses, a computer will have a shorter life expectancy without protection. I believe our minds are similar to computers: We need anti-virus software to protect our mental health.

You can purchase anti-virus software to guard against cyber viruses, but what does a person use to guard his or her mind? When a virus attacks a computer, the owner can download a program to clean the machine, but what can we do when our minds are breaking down and not functioning properly? I believe following the doctrine of the Scriptures gives the protection we need for our minds. As dangerous as it is to have a vulnerable computer, it is even more risky to have a mind with no protection in the form of the word of God. God's original plan and purpose was for humans to experience peace of mind.

Could it be that despite Adam and Eve's disobedience, they had previously been so accustomed to peace that they immediately could not handle experiencing negative emotions such as shame and guilt? Not only did they swiftly recognize that there was a change in their normal level of mental and emotional functioning, but they were willing to accept the provision of God to re-stabilize their minds. Fortunately for them, there was no other help offered than that of God, so the choice was easy. Today, many needing mental health assistance are encouraged to turn to the help of psychologists, psychiatrists, therapists or other licensed mental health practitioners, as opposed to Scriptures, prayer and faith in God.

A Personal Experience with
Faith and Mental Health

———————

Early in my career, I worked at an outpatient mental health facility that specialized in serving children and youth. I recall one family in particular that responded well to faith-based treatment. The case was originally referred to me as a result of the youngest males aggression and increased suspension rate at school. In the course of treatment, my client's mother acknowledged that she and her family had relocated to the Western New York area a few years ago and was not attending church, as they had in their former state of residence. While there were undeniable triggers to my client's anger within the home that he could not improve as a child, the mother's motivation to make those changes weakened when she was not actively attending church. Once this was brought to my attention, the mother and I began discussing churches the family could attend in their neighborhood. As a result of the positive impact attending church had on the family dynamics, I would on occasion transport them to and from church services. The mother reported that psychotherapy, medication management or classifying the child with special education services was not enough to manage his behavior. This family needed to have their connection of faith re-established. I am intrigued and wonder how many children in my previous client's situation will go from counselor to counselor and/or be prescribed a variety or mediations or worse yet be misdiagnosed, in part because the helper(s) would not acknowledge the value of integrating faith when treating mental health.

CHAPTER 4

The Impact of Research in the Social Sciences

Medical science is a respected field because of the many tangible results it has afforded society. With a desire to gain similar validation, disciplines in the social sciences such as psychology attempted to develop scientific methods within the scope of their practice. But, the very elements of what medical science prides itself on such as causal hypotheses and replicable procedures that give way to conclusive findings would prove arduous for the social sciences to mimic. Social sciences tend to rely more on subjective rather than objective data. To put it another way, psychological researchers are unable to accurately assess someone else's psyche with definitive claims on their findings, because it is impossible to totally know another person's mind.

> "The heart is deceitful above all things, and it is exceedingly perverse and corrupt and severely, mortally sick! Who can know it [perceive, understand, be acquainted with his own heart and mind]?" (Jer. 17:9).

However, this is not necessarily the case for medical researchers, as they are not studying subjective elements. When your doctor asks what your blood type is, he or she does not have to depend only on your answer. He or she can actually perform an analysis to determine your exact blood type. Medical researchers that are seeking treatment for cancer or Alzheimer's can conduct experiments on animals. They will make a hypothesis that whatever treatment they are manipulating will have a significant impact on the cancer. The effectiveness of the treatment can be measured in tangible ways that can have little to do with the patient's mental health status. Subsequently, there is less reliance on human reporting and more emphasis on measureable data.

Psychological research is more dependent on what the evaluator interprets from the person he or she is studying. So, at best, psychological researchers can attest to the high correlation of a relationship, as opposed to determining causation. This does not mean that psychological researchers cannot conduct research and provide valid conclusions; rather, my point is that in general their findings and discussions will be significantly less conclusive when compared to medical research or to other disciplines that have more objective methods. Take, for instance, an example below of a simple psychological research study.

First, I will introduce some basic terminology. In research, the independent variable (IV) is considered the force being manipulated, while the dependent variable (DV) is the measureable outcome. In my research example, the IV will be the hours a student uses to study and the DV will be the grades the student obtains. I will make an unassuming hypothesis: The more a student studies, the better his or her grades will be. If I were a psychological researcher, I would propose that increased study time has a positive correlation or linear relationship with improved grades. In other words, both variables are increasing as opposed to one increasing while the other is decreasing.

To actually determine the accuracy of this hypothesis, I would administer a self- report measure or examine the students' subsequent test grades. While this claim is more likely true than not, there are still extraneous variables not accounted for that could also be impacting the suggested relationship we see between the IV and the DV. For instance, a particular student's teacher could have changed his or her teaching style which provided a more successful learning environment. In other words, the student could have been paying more attention in class, since the teacher was communicating the subject more effectively. Subsequently, increased attention could actually be the reason for the rise in grade performance as opposed to the additional time spent studying. If the student's grades improved by some force other than study time, an extraneous or confounding variable would better explain or account for the change.

It is true that extraneous variables have the potential to be present in any type of research project (whether it falls within the hard or social sciences), but they have a greater impact in less controlled studies where many influences are present. Controlled studies allow the researcher to have as much control as possible over extraneous variables that could be responsible for the DV outcome, other than the identified IV of the study. Uncontrolled studies can therefore be significantly less conclusive. Even so, psychological researchers have made significant contributions and, when ethical, do utilize controlled studies. My point, however, is that psychological research is not a precise science because it deals with feelings and thoughts, which can be impacted by many extraneous variables. It is impossible to know with precision what another person is thinking and feeling as well as the unconscious motives that underlie a behavior. Although I gave a simple research example to introduce the role of research in psychology, let's consider a more convoluted case.

A clinical social worker is working on a murder case along with a forensic serologist and both want to obtain information regarding the case to assist with the prosecution. The mental health professional is seeking to obtain the mental health status and the serologist wants to examine the blood type of the accused. Both professionals are essentially trying to establish that the accused is the actual perpetrator. The clinical social worker would use a variety of best-practice therapeutic techniques to assist with obtaining information such as a battery of mental health assessments, administration of various questionnaires and psychoanalysis. She would then compile a report and present it to the lead prosecutor and possibly serve as an "expert witness" during the trial. The steps the social worker or psychologist or other trusted mental health professional would perform are different from that of a forensic serologist.

Once the blood has been drawn, the serologist will evaluate the blood type and allow it to be presented in court. The determination of the blood type provided by the serologist will conclusively identify if the accused is the actual perpetrator or not. When the prosecutor and other court officials are presented with all pertinent information on the case such as the police evidence that led to the arrest, possible interrogation information as well as the clinical mental health assessment, if the serologist states the blood from the crime scene does not match the detained individual, the defense attorney will have a valid argument to demand the release of the arrested individual. Even with contradicting information given by clinical reports and testimonies from possible witnesses, if the blood type is more conclusive, the incarceration of the alleged criminal will have to be re-examined. DNA evidence has made way for the release of many wrongly accused.

In a report posted to the Innocence Blog, on September 5, 2013, in January 1991, a jury convicted Jeffery Deskovic of 1st degree rape and 2nd degree murder. Sometime after Jeffery's conviction, his case was taken on by the Innocence Project. Additional DNA testing initiated by the Innocence Project not only cleared Mr. Deskovic, but also identified the actual murderer. To my point, all information used to convict Mr. Deskovic was no longer valid when the medical evidence proved he was not the guilty offender of the tragedy that befell the victim. While the contributions of the mental health assessment and various other supplemental reports can offer some meaning, it simply is not strong enough when compared to that of concrete medical findings.

Research in Psychology and Social Work

Given the fluctuating relevance of psychological research, why does it continue? Well, in part I believe it does so because as mentioned earlier, psychology wants to achieve the sort of reputation that medical and other hard sciences have assumed. I take the time to underscore the motivation for continued research by the social sciences despite its limitations because it relates to a fundamental reason why psychology has not turned more to the incorporation of faith in its academic curriculum, research orientation and intervention development.

The field of psychology is responsible for which theories of human behavior, psychological treatment and clinical research are accepted and implemented. Clinical social work relies heavily on psychology for its course development and training, so by default aligns with many of the anti-God and anti-religious sentiments thereof. Anti-God views are evident in comments from psychology founding fathers like Freud, as it was a known fact he viewed religion as a crutch. The clinical positioning of the field of social work, however, is in some ways contradictory to its own foundation. In looking at references below, we see similarities and differences between social work and psychology.

Similarities between Clinical Social Work and Psychology

Chart A

Clinical Social Work	Psychology
1. Provides mental health therapy for a spectrum of disorders	Provides mental health therapy for a spectrum of disorders
2. Uses theories of human behavior and/or systemic models in treatment	Uses theories of human behavior and/or evidence based models in treatment
3. Conducts research to make contributions to understanding human behavior	Conducts research to make contributions to understanding human behavior
4. Seeks validation in part as a respected field of study through research	Seek continued validation as a respected field of study through research

Differences between Clinical Social Work and Psychology

Chart B

Social Work	Psychology
1. Takes a systemic approach to treatment in solving the problems of the individual	Focus is on the individual as the source for the problem

2.	Origins in benevolence and charity that gave way to advocacy	Origins in experimental and clinical research
3.	Uses the ground-work of psychology for mental health theories	Independent of social work in its origin; developed theories of human behavior based on experiments
4.	Specializes in case management; helps link and refer clients to community resources	Historically, more training in research and related publications

Clinical Social Work Merged with Psychology

Keeping in mind the above charts as a reference, let's take a closer look at the foundations of both fields. Researchers or medical doctors such as William Wundt are considered "fathers" of psychology, whereas individuals such as Jane Adams who did not have medical backgrounds but who wanted to help disenfranchised people are considered pioneers of social work. In therapy, clinical social work is typically distinguished from psychology by the manner in which dysfunction is viewed. Psychology tends to examine dysfunction as internal to the individual, whereas social work examines problems within the systems that impact the individual. How did these two fields of discipline that have such different origins end up on a strikingly similar clinical path? In a sense, these fields could have merged together because they both seek to address issues related to human behavior. From the beginning, social work was conducted by way of charity homes that were similar to the shelters provided to the unfortunate by religious institutions. With that being said, although social work in theory appears to be more open to acknowledging the impact of faith and spirituality, it still has not matured to the point of fully incorporating Christian views into its curriculum, despite the fact that religious entities played major roles in the foundation of its existence. Sadly, social work straying away from its inherent faith-based foundation did not happen for no reason. In the 20th century, the social work movement began to secularize and distance itself from its religious basis in favor of that of utilitarianism.

Thus far, I have contrasted two social science fields that both address mental health functioning. In sum, for the "sake of progress" both entities have espoused a more scientific approach and thus rely less on incorporating matters of faith into practice. I am not suggesting that all social workers or psychologists or other scientists are anti-God; but what I am aiming to do is to establish the direction psychology and social work have taken as it relates to the development of mental health theory and intervention.

The questioning of the Bible began during the 17th-18th century as the scientific approach was developed and extended into the 19th century. For many scientists, because the existence of God cannot be proven, it is deemed probable that He does not exist or is not worth investigating. With that view in mind, it is easy to understand how one could draw the conclusion that if God does not exist, then certainly the Bible is useless or at best a mythical and/or historical document and undoubtedly a futile reference.

As previously stated, not all researchers, practitioners and scientists operate from an anti-God framework. In fact, there are researchers that use their faith to guide their scientific practice, such as Dr. Jobe Martin. Initially, Dr. Martin accepted anti-God views like evolution, proposed by Charles Darwin. Dr. Martin's perspective changed when he was challenged by his students to validate his belief in evolution and he embarked on a quest for knowledge. The discoveries he made changed his personal views and the way in which he practiced science. During Dr. Jobe's search to endorse his beliefs, he was surprised to discover that there was not any sensible evidence to support the anti-God views of evolution he once held dear.

Dr. Martin has since used his Christian faith to inform his scientific outlook. In his book, *The Evolution of a Creationist, A Laymen's Guide to the Conflict between The Bible and Evolutionary Theory*, Dr. Martin underscores the gaps in evolutionary theory and evidence. Dr. Jobe has pointed out that "as God's creatures, we do not subject the Bible-to science; we subject "science" to the Bible" (Martin 2002, 67). Dr. Martin has since written various publications that explain how nature speaks to the existence of God and how to integrate faith and science.

Dr. Martin and others demonstrate the fact that science does not have to be used against God, but rather, when the researcher is willing, science can be instrumental in demonstrating God's abilities. I do not make these later points to extract the value of science, as the contributions of scientists to the progress of practically every area of human life are invaluable and undoubtedly necessary. My point is that science and God can and should complement each other.

> "God delights in concealing things; scientists delight in discovering things" (Prov. 25:2, MSG).

Although there are a number of doctors and researchers that allow their faith in God to guide their scientific practice, many others do not. Unfortunately, many of the scientists who hold anti-God views have a more dominant influence on research and have thus shaped the course curriculum and subsequent clinical interventions in the fields of psychology and theories of human behavior used in social work.

A Personal Experience with
Faith and Mental Health:

Once when I was in college, I took an anthropology class and the instructor began talking about the history of past cultures and human life. Based on his interpretation of the evidence, the professor began attempting to discredit the existence of God. Instead of simply reporting the results of the research, once again the educational platform was used to promote anti-theocratic dogma. In one such class, I made it known that I did not agree with his expression and stated why as a Christian, I opposed his view.

Research and education do go hand in hand, as research can add to the body of knowledge in various growing areas of profession and inquiry. The results of research can allow any educator to provide information to students who are eager to learn. But, professors should not use the classroom to attack the faith of their students. Educators should not use their position as an excuse to condescend students who are secure and courageous enough to believe that science, research and education can support God.

If you are a student reading this, I would like to encourage you to hold fast to your Christian faith. Understand that although you attend your classes to receive knowledge on a particular subject matter, you do not have to succumb to the pressures to abandon or compromise your faith.

CHAPTER 5

Great Thinkers and
Their Contributions:

Psychoanalysis

In 2001, Time Magazine identified Freud as one of the most important thinkers of the last century. Freud was a man who publicly despised faith and did not promote any integration between faith and science in his work. In fact, Freud relied so heavily on the practice of science that he asserted that the advancement of society was not possible without it.

In the 21st Century, despite the known fact that many later psychoanalysts discredited Freud's theories for not being empirical, his work continues to have a place in the professional curriculum of training clinicians and theorists. I too give Freud credit for developing the theory of psychoanalysis, which attempts to discern the connection between peoples' unconscious thoughts and their manifested behavior. Freud's analysis of the mind into the classic three components of the Id, Ego and Superego is also brilliant. However, the major flaw in Freud's position is that he gives more credence to his views than to God's.

There are a variety of schools of thought in the field of psychology besides psychoanalysis, such as cognitive and evolutionary psychology, but for the purposes of this book I will be unable touch upon them all. However, I will address another leading school of thought, which is much different in practical implementation than psychoanalysis but has the same goal in mind of wanting to change human behavior. This school of thought is known as the behavioral approach.

Behaviorism

Burrhus Frederick Skinner, more commonly known as B.F. Skinner, made a name for himself with significant contributions to the field of psychology through his theories of operant conditioning and cognitive behavior therapy (CBT). Skinner, also the author of a novel entitled, *Walden Two*, describes an ideal community that exists where people are happy, creative and governed by reinforced behavior. During my years as an undergraduate, I remember thinking while hearing aspects of this novel taught "this place that Skinner is describing sure sounds like heaven in the Bible." Consider chart A below in a comparative analysis of Skinner's *Walden Two* against the apostle John's illustration of heaven and other biblical references.

Chart A

B.F. Skinner's Walden Two	Heaven as described in the Book of Revelation and God
Six day work week with one day off	God blessed the seventh day and rested from His work (Gen. 2:3, author's paraphrase)
Members are described as happy	Saints have comfort from negative emotions (Rev. 21:4, author's paraphrase)
There is a hierarchal governing system	There is a governing body (Rev. 4:10, author's paraphrase)
Acceptable behavior is rewarded	Individuals are rewarded for their works (Rev. 22:12, author's paraphrase)

Atheistic Views of Skinner and Freud

I use this chart as a comparison to illustrate that the construction of the utopian community Skinner imagined was devoid of religion which continues to carry the message that God is not needed. Freud actually viewed the perpetuation of reliance on faith and thus the Heavenly Father as a weakness in the individual. Yet, scripture informs us that the entire concept of fatherhood stems from the Heavenly Father.

> "…I bow my knees before the Father of our Lord Jesus Christ; For Whom every family in heaven and on earth is named [that Father from Whom all Fatherhood takes its title and derives its name]" (Eph. 3:14-15, authors paraphrase).

Based on Scripture, an individual would have a "longing for the Father," or as I have heard others refer to it, a "God-sized void," despite a fulfilled relationship with his or her biological father. Properly identifying the void the individual feels as a longing for the Father is not always achieved for every person. The individual may only experience a general sense of incompleteness or void in his or her life. Since there is a lack of understanding on their part as to what they truly need, the seeker may try to fill their need for a relationship with God and psychological development with futile efforts. For instance, they might try excessively to increase their wealth, abuse drugs, have multiple sexual relationships, become an academic "over achiever" or obsessively work extended hours on the job. You may identify with some of these behaviors in your own life. Attempting to replace the longing for a relationship with the Heavenly Father with a dysfunctional need for attachment emanating from an unfulfilled father-child relationship is a huge misconception on Freud's part and anyone who espouses that view.

In reality, Freud and Skinner also condescended individuals of faith when they alluded to faith in God as an intellectual weakness. However, research has shown variables such as education did not relate significantly to whether or not an individual with a psychiatric illness sought treatment of faith healing (Kar 2008, 735). The fact that there is no major difference in the level of education regarding treatment of mental health invalidates Freud and Skinner's demeaning opinion that ignorant and gullible people practice faith. In fact, we are starting to see more of a shift that views spirituality not as pathological but as conducive to addressing mental health issues (Dein et al. 2010, 63).

Philosophy, God and Plato

Psychology is not the only academic field that has had a deep-seated impact on today's thinking. Ancient philosophy certainly continues to influence much of Western culture to this day. Plato, a philosopher and protégé of Socrates, also examined the life of the mind. In a written piece of Plato's work, he theorizes that what we as humans experience from day-to-day life are imperfect forms replicated from their perfect counterparts. In other words, what we are exposed to through our senses (e.g., what we see or hear) are weaker forms or representations of their otherwise original or perfect state. According to his assessment, there is something more to the existence of objects beyond what is seen with the natural senses.

The Bible noted, before Plato, that in fact there is a connection between the visible and the invisible. The Bible makes it clear that Jesus was the visible replication of the Heavenly Father.

> "[Now] he is the exact likeness of the unseen God [the visible representation of the invisible]; He is the Firstborn of all creation" (Col. 1:15).

The Good Book further informs readers that certain aspects of heaven can be discerned through the works of men who were given instructions on how to make earthly reproductions. Scripture makes this known when discussing the temple and the duties of the priests in the temple:

> "[But these offer] service [merely] as a pattern and as a foreshadowing of [what has its true existence and reality in] the heavenly sanctuary. For when Moses was about to erect the tabernacle, he was warned by God,

saying, See to it that you make it all [exactly] according to the copy (the model) which was shown to you on the mountain" (Heb. 8:5).

In the Our Father Prayer, Jesus informs His disciples that when praying, we should ask for a replication of the Father's will on earth, as is being completed in the heavens.

"Pray, therefore, like this: Our Father Who is in heaven, hallowed (kept holy) be Your name. Your kingdom come, Your will be done on earth as it is in heaven" (Matt. 6:9-10).

The apostle Paul continues to confirm that beyond what human eyes can see, there are perfected and enduring forms:

"While we look not at the things which are seen, but at the things which are not seen: for the things which are seen are temporal; but the things which are not seen are eternal" (2nd Cor. 4:18, KJV).

Plato, therefore, had some correct insight when he asserted that the tangible natures of what is experienced daily in life are imperfect forms of original existence.

Plato and God on the Soul

Plato also attempted to describe the intangibilities of the human soul, although the Bible has already provided us with a full description. In some of his known works, Plato stated that the body and soul, two substances, separate at the moment of death. He asserted that as a result of the death process, the soul is liberated from its entrapment inside the body and goes to the place where the forms (all universal notions or concepts) exist. Plato does not provide a definitive stance on what ultimately happens to human souls once they are freed from the body.

Plato's end analysis suggests no God and no concluding judgment for the individual or soul as a result of the right and wrong he or she committed while here on earth. However, where Plato and others missed the mark in discussing the hereafter is that their theories were not based in the knowledge of God, since the Bible indicates that "all souls are mine" and He determines their ultimate fate (Ezek. 18:4 author's paraphrase). Based on God's revelation to the apostle Paul, we know exactly what occurs at the ultimate transition for Christian believers.

> "Take notice! I tell you a mystery (a secret truth, an event decreed by the hidden purpose or counsel of God). We shall not all fall asleep [in death], but we shall all be changed (transformed) in a moment, in the twinkling of an eye, at the [sound of the] last trumpet call. For a trumpet will sound, and the dead [in Christ] will be raised imperishable (free and immune from decay), and we shall be changed (transformed). For this perishable [part of us] must put on the imperishable [nature], and this mortal [part of us, this nature that is capable of dying] must put on immortality (freedom from death). And when this perishable puts on the imperishable and this that was capable of dying puts on freedom from death, then shall be fulfilled the Scripture that says,

Death is swallowed up (utterly vanquished forever) in and unto victory" (1 Cor. 15:51-54).

In a renowned dialogue between Socrates and Plato, the two were discussing how to determine the depth of human knowledge. They believed that knowledge was innate and needed to merely be elicited from the person. The philosophers suggested that we already know everything needed to navigate life; and to access this knowledge we need only remember what we know. Some branches of psychology assert the opposite of what Plato and Socrates put forth by suggesting humans are born with a blank slate, or in other words, no information available mentally at birth, a theory known as tabula rasa.

The two perspectives on how we learn can be summarized as follows: The belief that we need only "remember" versus the belief that we need only "learn." The Bible does also offer explanations of how to view human knowledge but also recognizes God's ability for illumination. Beyond what philosophers have suggested, the Bible makes a distinction between natural or secular knowledge and spiritual knowledge:

> "He has made everything beautiful in its time. He also has planted eternity in men's hearts and minds [a divinely implanted sense of a purpose working through the ages which nothing under the sun but God alone can satisfy], yet so that men cannot find out what God has done from the beginning to the end" (Eccl. 3:11).

This biblical reference allows us to understand that without God's permission, individuals will not be able to access the spiritual knowledge and insight God wants concealed.

Plato and the apostle Paul agree that the soul is immortal and separates from the body; however, they do differ in the way in which they view the soul's final destination. Plato proposes that all souls go to a universal place, while John the Revelator reports that individuals whose names were not written in the book of life or who rejected Jesus Christ as Savior will experience the second death (the first death would be the initial, physical death), which is ultimately being cast into the lake of fire in hell.

"Then death and Hades (the state of death or disembodied existence) were thrown into the lake of fire. This is the second death, the lake of fire. And if anyone's [name] was not found recorded in the Book of Life, he was hurled into the lake of fire" (Rev. 20:14-15).

A Personal Experience with Faith and Mental Health:

Making significant contributions can be a vital aspect of one's career. I specifically recall making a proposal to the CEO of a mental health facility regarding the need for increased visibility of services within certain communities. Initially, I marketed within the faith-based community, and the response was overwhelmingly positive. A leading person in the faith-based community expressed gratitude for my efforts to bridge the gap between people of faith and mental health. Later, she disclosed she had a loved-one who struggled with such an illness and had wished that this type of service was not so taboo, in times past.

I found it important as a Christian, servant of the Gospel and practicing social worker to demonstrate the compatibility of all three roles, as I was able to provide direct therapy to some of the families I recruited. Families of Christian faith were able to experience receiving mental health therapy from not only a trained professional, but more importantly one who was in agreement with their core value of faith. I can honestly say that for many of those referred families, my ability to integrate their faith in therapy contributed to their ability to remain engaged.

CHAPTER 6

What Does the Bible Say About Mental Health?

The Bible has much to say about the functioning of the mind and mental health; but those who choose not to accept God or the Bible might be significantly less likely to apply God's recommendation for improving their mental health. Yet, according to Scripture, only true and lasting peace can come from God. In terms of understanding mental health from a biblical perspective, I will give a brief description expounding on the message of the Bible.

The Bible is separated into two eras; Before Christ (BC) also known as the Old Testament (OT) and in the Year of Our Lord (AD) or the New Testament (NT). After the fall of Adam and Eve, their nature became sinful and this nature was passed on to all humans. As we read earlier, the first couple tried to resolve their feelings of guilt by making clothes to cover their nakedness. The relief Adam and Eve were seeking was peace of mind and since that time all human beings have been searching for a way to obtain genuine peace of mind.

Subsequent to Adam and Eve's fall, for a certain timeframe in the OT, God allowed mankind to try and obtain a sense of peace and ease with God by performing various forms of atonement. OT priests would go into the sacred temple to sacrifice animals and then offer that blood for atonement to God. In providing these sacrifices, forgiveness of sins was to be granted; however, what these sacrifices did not accomplish was purification of the minds of the sinners. The failure of these kinds of atonements to offer lasting peace in the OT served as an indication in the NT that we need something greater than our sacrifices to obtain God's pardon from sin and receive peace and tranquility of soul.

"...under this system, the gifts and sacrifices can't really get to the heart of the matter, can't assuage the conscience of the people, but are limited to matters of ritual and behavior. It's essentially a temporary arrangement until a complete overhaul can be made" (Heb. 9:9, MSG, author's paraphrase).

The fact that God initially required the killing of animals was not a contradiction on His behalf; rather, it served as a prophetic indication for the need of Jesus Christ as Savior. In permitting OT sacrifices, God was proving that the blood of animals would never be able to fully redeem us from sin, just as the fig garments Adam and Eve made were unable to remove the sense of guilt that robbed them of their peace. Jesus Christ dying on the cross was deemed as the ultimate sacrifice and therefore, according to the NT, it is faith and obedience in and to Christ that affords believers peace with God. Accepting Jesus Christ as Lord and Savior is therefore the only way to access the type of peace that is lasting. Understanding that true peace from and with God can only be obtained through faith in Christ is a critical point, since many individuals are seeking peace in alternative forms of mental health treatment such as medication and psychotherapy. Consider the words of Christ regarding peace:

"Peace I leave with you; My [own] peace I now give and bequeath to you. Not as the world gives do I give to you..." (John 14:27, author's paraphrase).

In taking a closer look at this Scripture, we can see that two types of peace are being compared. First mentioned is the peace that comes from God and second is the peace that comes from the world or without God. Jesus makes the distinction to say that His divine peace is different from secular peace. Some Bibles describe secular peace as being fragile or easily broken and damaged; however, the actual type of peace in the original Hebrew context from this Scripture is actually described as being joined to or set as one again. In other words, only the peace that comes from God can set our minds right and restore calmness.

Representations of Peace in the Old and New Testament

Whether we are viewing Scripture from an OT or NT perspective, disobedience can be connected to poor mental health.

OT	NT
"The Lord will afflict you with madness, blindness and confusion of mind…the sights you see will drive you mad…until you are destroyed…there the Lord will give you an anxious mind, eyes weary with longing, and a despairing heart… the Lord will also bring on you every kind of sickness and disaster not recorded in this Book of the Law, until you are destroyed." (Deut. 28:28, 34, 65, 61, author's paraphrase).	"Now as he traveled on, he came near to Damascus, and suddenly a light from heaven flashed around him, and he fell to the ground …trembling and astonished…he got up from the ground, but though his eyes were opened, he could see nothing… and he was unable to see for three days, and he neither ate nor drank [anything]" (Acts 9:3-4, 6, 8-9, author's paraphrase).

While it is true that some of the manners in which God dealt with people differed between the OT and the NT, I purposefully use Scriptures from both testaments to speak to the fact that mental health issues, on occasion, can be types of divine retribution for sin. In The OT reference, God warns of the type of difficulties the Israelites would encounter if they choose to disobey Him after He had blessed them. Undoubtedly, we see that mental health calamities would and did befall individuals who choose to disobey God.

As you read this, you maybe thinking that these types of consequences seem unbelievable or unfair for a loving God to place upon his creation. However, peace is a gift from God and He alone decides how it is dispersed. If someone willfully rejects the truth of His word, God is justified in removing a sense of ease and clam from that individual. The Bible therefore informs us that if we desire peace, we have a responsibility to obey the word. For example, if you were or are an employer, would you pay your employees indefinitely if they did not fulfill their job descriptions? No, because their financial compensation is a reward for their labor. So in a sense, peace of mind is a reward from God to those who trust and are in right standing with Him based on their obedient actions. When the dust settles, God is not obligated to dispense His peace for any other circumstances beyond obedience to His word, as it is in "serving God that acceptance and approval from God" is given (Rom. 14:17, author's paraphrase).

> God's word also states, "You will guard and keep him in perfect and constant peace whose mind [both its inclination and its character] is stayed on You, because he commits himself to You, leans on You, and hopes confidently in You" (Isa. 26:3).

Bridging the Gap between the Bible and Mental Health Treatment

By this point, it should be clear that I affirm the position that mental health therapists need to have increased exposure to and proficient knowledge of how the Bible links disobedience to poor mental health and psychotic behavior. What is more, clinicians do not have to be clergy members to incorporate biblically-based assessments and interventions when it is clinically appropriate. In continuing to emphasize the connection between mental health presentations and faith, I would now like to provide three individuals from the Bible as sample case studies.

Case Study of Nebuchadnezzar

In the Bible, Nebuchadnezzar was King of Babylon. According to Scripture, this King became overly prideful and as a result, a type of mental illness befell him.

> "The king said, Is not this the great Babylon that I have built as the royal residence and seat of government by the might of my power and for the honor and glory of my majesty? While the words were still in the king's mouth, there fell a voice from heaven, saying, O king Nebuchadnezzar, to you it is spoken: The kingdom has departed from you, And you shall be driven from among men and your dwelling will be with the living creatures of the field. You will be made to eat grass like the oxen, and seven times [or years] shall pass over you until you have learned and know that the Most High

[God] rules in the kingdom of men and gives it to whomever He will" (Dan. 4:30-32).

Reference A

1- Nebuchadnezzar thought like an animal (Dan. 4:16, author's paraphrase).
2- The King ate grass and lived with the animals (Dan. 4:25, 33, author's paraphrase).

There have been various postulations regarding the specific condition Nebuchadnezzar suffered from as outlined in this passage. For the focus of this book, however, my assertion is that his condition was instigated by God as opposed to secular causes. In 2014, if King Nebuchadnezzar were mandated to or voluntarily sought treatment, he would be given psychotropic medication and some form of cognitive behavior therapy (CBT). While these interventions could have helped improve his functioning, they do, however, evade the etiology for the onset of his psychosis.

Case Study of King Saul

The next case study focuses on the first King of Israel, Saul. Saul was a man who was chosen by the Israelites to be their King, although the Israelites were warned by the prophet Samuel that Saul would prove to be an unsuitable choice. The onset of Saul's mental illness came about when he became jealous of the recognition that David, his son-in-law, received after a battle they both fought in. Saul's mind eventually became tormented to the point where he went insane, and he tried to kill any and everyone who would not side with him, including his son, Jonathan.

> "As they were coming home, when David returned from killing the Philistine, the women came out of all the Israelite towns, singing and dancing, to meet King Saul with timbrels, songs of joy, and instruments of music. And the women responded as they laughed and frolicked, saying, Saul has slain his thousands, and David his ten thousands. And Saul was very angry, for the saying displeased him; and he said, They have ascribed to David ten thousands, but to me they have ascribed only thousands. What more can he have but the kingdom? And Saul [jealously] eyed David from that day forward. The next day an evil spirit from God came mightily upon Saul, and he raved [madly] in his house, while David played [the lyre] with his hand, as at other times; and there was a Javelin in Saul's hand. And Saul cast the Javelin, for he thought, I will pin David to the wall. And David evaded him twice" (1 Sam. 18:6-11).

Reference B

1- "Saul was obsessively threatened by David's abilities and wanted to kill David and anyone who Saul thought might interfere with him killing David" (1 Sam. 18:10-11; 1 Sam. 19:1; 1 Sam. 22:17-18, author's paraphrase).

2- "Saul attached himself to any courageous people that he came across" (1 Sam. 14:52, author's paraphrase).

3- "Saul had a need for people's approval" (1 Sam. 13:11; 1 Sam. 15:24, 30, author's paraphrase).

4- "Saul wanted David to marry his daughter as a ploy" (1 Sam. 18:17, author's paraphrase).

5- "Saul was jealous of the acknowledgement David received" (1 Sam. 18:6-9, author's paraphrase).

There is additional information in the Bible regarding the onset of Saul's illness, such as the fact that God informed Saul that because of his disobedience, God was going to remove him as King over Israel. This foreknowledge gave way to paranoia, which Saul projected onto David. An important point to consider when thinking about the reason for Saul's mental illness is that, like Nebuchadnezzar, God brought about his illness because of the pride in Saul's heart.

Case Study of Judas Iscariot

The last case study I will use is that of Judas Iscariot, the betrayer of Jesus Christ. In Scripture, we see that Judas was a disciple selected by Jesus Himself. Prior to his following Christ, Judas was a thief and remained one while with Christ and the other disciples. After Judas, also known as the Son of Perdition, betrayed Jesus, Judas experienced a state of mental anguish which led to Judas's ultimate demise.

> "When it was morning, all the chief priests and the elders of the people held a consultation against Jesus to put Him to death; And they bound Him and led Him away and handed Him over to Pilate the governor. When Judas, His betrayer, saw that [Jesus] was condemned, [Judas was afflicted in mind and troubled for his former folly; and] with remorse [with little more than a selfish dread of the consequences] he brought back the thirty pieces of silver to the chief priests and the elders, Saying, I have sinned in betraying innocent blood. They replied, What is that to us? See to that yourself. And casting the pieces of sliver [forward] into the [Holy Place of the sanctuary of the] temple, he departed; and he went off and hanged himself" (Matt. 27:1-5).

Reference C

1- "Judas was pilfering from the collections/donations from the ministry" (St. John 12:6, author's paraphrase).
2- "Judas requested a reward for betraying Jesus and thus handing Him over to His enemies" (Matt. 26:15-16, 47-48, author's paraphrase).

Had Judas Iscariot presented in a modern clinician's office and expressed his desire to commit suicide, he would probably be placed on a suicide watch and given a suicide contract. Judas would also likely receive a psychiatric evaluation, be prescribed antidepressant medication and receive psychotherapy. While utilizing these interventions would not necessarily be inappropriate, I argue that exclusively employing these interventions circumvents the underlying spiritual component of the illness. A curse had befallen Judas because of the grave sin he committed in betraying Jesus:

> "...and not one of them has perished or is lost except the son of perdition [Judas Iscariot-the one who is now doomed to destruction, destined to be lost], that the Scripture might be fulfilled" (John 17:12, author's paraphrase).

Allow me to clarify this reference to curses and suicide. I make it known that Judas was cursed when he committed suicide not to demonize anyone suffering with suicidal thoughts or mental illness. I have had close personal relationships with people who, unfortunately, committed suicide. Yet, I also cannot deny the biblical reality that there are some people who are demon-possessed or under the influence of demonic spirits and present with a variety of mental health issues that can be misdiagnosed and ultimately treated improperly. The Bible is replete with examples of individuals who clearly have emotional, psychological and behavioral issues that needed deliverance from God. Consider the below description of an individual who was demon-possessed, who, if placed in a psychiatric ward today, would possibly fail to be given a comprehensive psychosocial assessment that fully addresses the realities of the faith component:

> "They sailed on to the country of the Gerasenes, directly opposite Galilee. As he stepped out onto land, a madman from town met him; he was a victim of

demons. He hadn't worn clothes for a long time, nor lived at home; he lived in the cemetery. When he saw Jesus he screamed, fell before him, and bellowed, "What business do you have messing with me? You're Jesus, Son of the High God, but don't give me a hard time!" (The man said this because Jesus had started to order the unclean spirit out of him.) Time after time the demon threw the man into convulsions. He had been placed under constant guard and tied with chains and shackles, but crazed and driven wild by the demon, he would shatter the bonds" (Luke 8:26-29, MSG).

When providing treatment to individuals with mental health issues, I am not suggesting that the foregoing of medication is a best practice in every instance. Coming from the heart of this book is the message that faith and the Bible should have a leading role in mental health treatment when this combination of approaches is appropriate. The use of these biblical references and case studies is not meant to provide a "Bible lesson." The purpose instead is to 1) emphasize that with balanced training and information, mental health clinicians can gain an awareness of potential faith-based perspectives that might be of use to the clients they provide services to, and 2) possibly consider joint therapy with a pastor or clergy person to address the realities of underlying biblical issues.

A Personal Experience with
Faith and Mental Health:

When I was approximately 21 years old, I was attending college. I can vividly remember sitting at a computer doing data entry for my work-study job when suddenly my mind was bombarded with the most hideous, blasphemous thoughts about God. Although I was not experiencing auditory hallucinations, these thoughts were certainly obsessive and intrusive. The speed of those repetitious thoughts was incredibly overwhelming. I felt like a flood of horror had taken over my mind. The only thing I could think to do was stop typing and speak out of my mouth "the blood of Jesus, the blood of Jesus." I did this because, according to the Bible, it took the shedding of Christ's blood to redeem mankind:

> "And they have overcome (conquered) him by means
> of the blood of the Lamb and by the utterance of their
> testimony..." (Rev. 12:11, author's paraphrase).

So although my mind was in turmoil, I knew that one way to deal with that issue was to recite the word of God. These thoughts continued beyond this one incident, and I found myself feeling alone because I found it embarrassing to discuss. Eventually, the theme of those obsessive thoughts ceased, but then new ones arose. As a result, I continued to suffer psychologically. Over a period of time, I began discussing the nature of those thoughts with trusted loved ones and friends. At one time, I contemplated seeking professional assistance when the pressures of life seemed to be enveloping me, but I also continued attending church services. After attending one particular church service, I felt alleviation and hope. While the mental torment did not go away altogether after that point, I am glad that my faith was able to carry me through. Hope is what the Bible offers through faith in God. My hope and trust has brought me to a place where I currently do not experience the same type of mental pressures that I did at one time. Hope for change is not necessarily offered from the medical model in treating mental illness. I found that the more I practiced my faith, wholeheartedly, the less mental distress I experienced.

CHAPTER 7

Proposed Interventions for Addressing Mental Health Issues in Practice

Although I have previously offered a working definition of mental health, I now turn to the most critical issue of this book, which is the development of faith-based courses trainings and interventions for treating mental illness. The overwhelming point to be made is this: If clinicians, researchers, educators and others do not permit the incorporation of faith into the spectrum of clinical practice, only incomplete assessments and services can be implemented. I believe one of the benefits of implementing faith-based interventions for believers and those clients who are open to the Christian perspective is the potential for decreasing recidivism.

The Mind of the Client

From a biblical perspective, humans are considered, to be a type of trinity in that we are three-dimensional. We possess a body (physical shell), soul (mind, will and emotions) and spirit (life force and/or nature). When an individual receives mental health counseling, the therapist is attempting to change or modify the soul or mind, since we desire to change or alter the person's thinking to improve his or her behavior.

The words of Christ have the ability to divinely convert the spirits of earnest listeners and readers, which then leads way to sustained mental health, once the mind is renewed.

> "It is the Spirit Who gives life [He is the Life-giver]; the flesh conveys no benefit whatever [there is no profit in it]. The words (truths) that I have been speaking to you are spirit and life" (John 6:63).

> "The law of the Lord is perfect, restoring the [whole] person; the testimony of the Lord is sure, making wise the simple" (Psalms 19:7).

Depending on the type of words that the professional uses and the client's ability to be involved and engaged in the therapeutic process, the client's soul or mind may change. However, the individual who internalizes truth in counseling presented in the form of the Bible also has the opportunity to receive the spirit of God, which allows for the maintenance of the presumably appropriate change identified in counseling.

An Example of Mental Health and the Heart

In the final hours of convicted serial killer Ted Bundy's life, he had an interview with noted Bible scholar, Dr. James Dobson. During this interview, Bundy acknowledges that despite his admission of being raised in a Christian home and attending church with his family, a sinister obsession to kill grew within him. In Bundy's own words, his over-indulgence in violent pornography significantly contributed to his deviant behavior. He acknowledges, however, that as a result of the Christian doctrine he had been exposed to while growing up, he initially tried to inhibit his impulse to murder, but eventually overcame those convictions. Exposure to the truth is the first step in changing the heart but the second step is just as essential: One must receive a new heart and accept Jesus Christ as Savior. So although Bundy had been exposed to the truth, he clearly had not received a new nature or spirit during the time in which he was committing murder, because one cannot practice sin if one has received a new spirit from God.

A change in spirit prompted by faith in Christ is what actually promotes a change in behavior and leads to the individual obtaining peace. It is therefore my opinion that many clinicians are fighting a losing battle when they try to establish a permanent change within the client without using the words of Christ. We clinicians try to help our clients based on our education, personal and professional experience, but because we are flawed we lack the ability to change people's hearts. Hearing, believing and accepting the Gospel of Jesus Christ is the only method available to not only divinely change a soul, but also to convert the spirit. In other words, while the clinician is working on changing the person's mind for the better, the individual's spirit may still be corrupted and lack the ability to sustain change, or worse yet, digress even farther from a path pleasing to God.

One of the reasons a change in heart or nature is necessary is because this new nature prevents a person from permanently abiding in sin:

> "No one born (begotten) of God [deliberately, knowing, and habitually] practices sin, for God's nature abides in him [His principle of life, the divine sperm, remains permanently within him]; and he cannot practice sinning because he is born (begotten) of God" (1 John 3:9). In short, accepting the words of Christ that change the spirit is considered being a born-again Christian.

> "Jesus answered him, I assure you, most solemnly I tell you, that unless a person is born again (anew, from above), he cannot ever see (know, be acquainted with, and experience) the kingdom of God. Nicodemus said to Him, How can a man be born when he is old? Can he enter his mother's womb again and be born? Jesus answered, I assure you, most solemnly I tell you, unless a man is born of water and [even] the Spirit, he cannot [ever] enter the kingdom of God. What is born of [from] the flesh is flesh [of the physical is physical]; and what is born of the Spirit is spirit. Marvel not [do not be surprised, astonished] at My telling you, You must all be born anew (from above)" (John 3:3-7).

Many individuals resist accepting the authority of God's word by giving some of the following excuses:

1. Attending church or temple is sufficient; this makes me right in God's eyes; I don't need to practice any life-style change the Bible may advise.
2. God understands human nature and therefore the behaviors I want to engage in are permissible by my own discretion.
3. There is no one that is perfect, so why try to fulfill a certain standard?

For the excuse makers, Jesus makes it clear that if you love Him, you will not be satisfied with continually committing behaviors that He disapproves of.

> "If you [really] love Me, you will keep (obey) My commandments" (John 14:15).

It is therefore through practicing the Scriptures that we are able to lead better lives, because when our souls or minds are exposed to the word of God on a regular basis, it produces a life- changing impact. This impact is better experienced by individuals who sincerely approach God and His word in faith, as opposed to those with a cynical, unbelieving attitude.

Although there will be many who accept the Gospel of Jesus Christ, there will be many who do not. The Bible offers an explanation of why those individuals do not accept the truth:

> "But even if our Gospel (the glad tidings) also be hidden (obscured and covered up with a veil that hinders the knowledge of God), it is hidden [only] to those who are

perishing and obscured [only] to those who are spiritually dying and veiled [only] to those who are lost. For the god of this world has blinded the unbelievers' minds [that they should not discern the truth], preventing them from seeing the illuminating light of the Gospel of the glory of Christ (the Messiah), Who is the Image and Likeness of God" (2 Cor. 4:3-4).

Proposed Biblical Interventions for Confession and Meditation

The interventions that I put forth to be used in treatment involve incorporating Scripture into therapy by way of developing manuals that are biblically based that would speak to the particular needs of the client receiving therapy. Chart B below will provide examples of thought-replacement techniques clients can use, based upon the issue he or she may be facing. In so doing, this allows for a type of mind renewal. According to the Bible, it is necessary for the mind to be renewed, and it is therefore fitting to have specific Scriptures incorporated into therapy that speak to the exact issue the client is struggling with. Transforming the mind in all areas is also a biblical instruction:

> "Do not be conformed to this world (this age), [fashioned after and adapted to its external, superficial customs], but be transformed (changed) by the [entire] renewal of your mind [by its new ideals and its new attitude]… "(Romans 12:2).

It is necessary for the mind to be renewed to please God, because in renewing the mind the person presumably abandons his or her own way of thinking that is contrary to God's. The thoughts, images and impulses that come natural to us as humans are often offensive to God and when unmanaged can certainly cause us to develop mental and physical health problems. Consider the below Scripture that explains the way we humans think and behave when our minds or souls are not renewed according to the Bible.

> "...What comes out of a man is what makes a man unclean and renders [him] unhallowed. For from within, [that is] out of the hearts of men, come base and wicked thoughts, sexual immorality, stealing, murder and adultery, coveting (a greedy desire to have more wealth), dangerous and destructive wickedness, deceit; unrestrained (indecent) conduct; an evil eye (envy), slander (evil speaking, malicious misrepresentation, abusiveness), pride (the sin of an uplifted heart against God and man), foolishness (folly, lack of sense, recklessness, thoughtlessness). All these evil [purposes and desires] come from within, and they make the man unclean and render him unhallowed" (Mark 7:20-23, author's paraphrase).

Chart A represents a biblical list of mental dysfunctions. While this list is not intended to be exhaustive, it offers additional references to biblical representations of mental health issues. Chart B shows examples of the types of Scriptures a well-informed clinician can use to aid his or her client in replacing faulty thinking while providing therapeutic services.

Chart A

Biblical Examples of Psychological
and Mental Distress

Possible manifestations of trauma: Mutism	"You hold my eyes from closing; I am so troubled that I cannot speak" (Ps. 77:4).
Possible manifestations of schizophrenia: Delusions (positive symptoms)	"So I also will choose their delusions *and* mockings, their calamities *and* afflictions, and I will bring their fears upon them—because when I called, no one answered; when I spoke, they did not listen *or* obey. But they did what was evil in My sight and chose that in which I did not delight" (Isa. 66:4). "So [it was] during supper, Satan having already put the thought of betraying Jesus in the heart of Judas Iscariot, Simon's son" (John 13:2).

Possible manifestations of depression and/or mood disorder(s):	"For the enemy has persecuted my soul; He has crushed my life to the ground; He has made me dwell in darkness, Like those who have long been dead. Therefore my spirit is overwhelmed within me; My heart within me is distressed" (Ps. 143:3-4, NKJV). "Those who sat in darkness and in the shadow of death, Bound in affliction and irons-Because they rebelled against the words of God, And despised the counsel of the Most High" (Ps. 107:10-11, NKJV).
Sleep loss	"I am sleepless *and* lie awake [mourning], like a bereaved sparrow alone on the housetop" (Ps. 102:7). "For they cannot sleep unless they have caused trouble *or* vexation; their sleep is taken away unless they have caused someone to fall" (Prov. 4:16).
Depression/general sadness	"Hope deferred makes the heart sick, but when the desire is fulfilled, it is a tree of life" (Prov. 13:12). "Therefore is my spirit overwhelmed and faints within me [wrapped in gloom]; my heart within my bosom grows numb" (Ps. 143:4).

Physical illness	"A calm *and* undisturbed mind *and* heart are the life *and* health of the body, but envy, jealousy, *and* wrath are like rottenness of the bones" (Prov. 14:30).
Anxiety	"In the multitude of my [anxious] thoughts within me, Your comforts cheer *and* delight my soul!" (Ps. 94:19). "Anxiety in a man's heart weighs it down, but an encouraging word makes it glad" (Prov. 12:25).
Appetite loss	"My heart is smitten like grass and withered, so that [in absorption] I forget to eat my food" (Ps. 102:4).

Chart B

Biblical Thought-Replacement Scriptures

Personality	"May He grant you out of the rich treasury of His glory to be strengthened *and* reinforced with mighty power in the inner man by the [Holy] Spirit [Himself indwelling your innermost being and personality]" (Eph. 3:16).
Healthy thinking that is biblically based	"The Lord knows the thoughts of man, that they are vain (empty and futile—only a breath). Blessed (happy, fortunate, to be envied) is the man whom You discipline *and* instruct, O Lord, and teach out of Your law" (Ps. 94:11-12). "For the weapons of our warfare are not physical [weapons of flesh and blood], but they are mighty before God for the overthrow and destruction of strongholds, [inasmuch as we] refute arguments and theories and reasonings and every proud and lofty thing that sets itself up against the [true] knowledge of God; and we lead every thought and purpose away captive into the obedience of Christ (the Messiah, the Anointed One)" (2 Cor. 10:4-5).

Forgiveness and healing	"Who forgives [every one of] all your iniquities, Who heals [each one of] all your diseases" (Ps. 103:3). "If we [freely] admit that we have sinned and confess our sins, He is faithful and just (true to His own nature and promises) and will forgive our sins [dismiss our lawlessness] and [continuously] cleanse us from all unrighteousness [everything not in conformity to His will in purpose, thought, and action]" (1 John 1:9).
Peace	"And He shall be a sanctuary [a sacred and indestructible asylum to those who reverently fear and trust in Him]"... (Isa. 8:14). "Because of and through the heart of tender mercy and loving-kindness of our God, a Light from on high will dawn upon us and visit [us] to shine upon and give light to those who sit in darkness and in the shadow of death, to direct and guide our feet in a straight line into the way of peace" (Luke 1:78-79).
Joy	"A happy heart is good medicine *and* a cheerful mind works healing, but a broken spirit dries up the bones" (Prov. 17:22).

General thought regulation	"For the rest, brethren, whatever is true, whatever is worthy of reverence *and* is honorable *and* seemly, whatever is just, whatever is pure, whatever is lovely *and* lovable, whatever is kind *and* winsome *and* gracious, if there is any virtue *and* excellence, if there is anything worthy of praise, think on *and* weigh *and* take account of these things [fix your minds on them]" (Phil. 4:8). "…abide in My word [holdfast to My teachings and live in accordance with them], you are truly My disciples. And you will know the Truth, and the Truth will set you free" (John 8:31-32, author's paraphrase).

A Practical Example of how Faith-Based Interventions Can Be Used In Mental Health Therapy

I can recall working with a young man at a former place of employment who had been diagnosed with schizoaffective disorder. I worked in collaboration with his psychiatrist at the same facility. In evaluating this youth's future, the psychiatrist stated to me that neither the youth nor the family should expect for the youth's hallucinations to ever cease during his lifetime: the most the family could hope for was the client to respond positively to psycho-education to help him deal with the hallucinations and medication management. As a therapist interested in faith-based interventions, I disagreed with that psychiatrist's position, and did state this directly to her.

In my sessions with the family we discussed faith and the client's mother reported that attending church provided a sense of hope for both her and the client. The client informed me that he felt better upon reading and reciting the 23rd Psalms, as his hallucinations minimized when doing so. In addition to reading the Bible, this client was occasionally being transported to a local church by his case manager, which the client enjoyed. An example of my client expressing his success with using Scriptures in his therapeutic process follows.

Therapist: How are you today?

Client: Good (mumbles additional words under his breath)

Therapist: It seems like you are whispering something. Would you like to tell me what thoughts you are experiencing?

Client: No (as he continues to mumble). He then gently hits his head with his hand.

Therapist: Are you hitting your head because you are trying to stop thinking bad thoughts?

Client: (nods his head up and down to indicate yes)

Therapist: Have you been reading the Bible? I know you said that helps you.

Client: Um, yes.

Therapist: Can you tell me what you read?

Client: The LORD is my shepherd; I shall not want. He maketh me to lie down in green pastures: he leadeth me beside the still waters. He restoreth my soul: he leadeth me in the paths of righteousness for his name's sake. Yea, though I walk through the valley of the shadow of death, I will fear no evil: for thou art with me; thy rod and thy staff they comfort me. Thou preparest a table before me in the presence of mine enemies: thou anointest my head with oil; my cup runneth over. Surely goodness and mercy shall follow me all the days of my life: and I will dwell in the house of the LORD forever.

Therapist: Wow. I see you have memorized the complete division of the 23rd Psalm. Does remembering these verses help you feel safe?

Client: Um, yes.

In actual practice, for the client who is open to discussing faith in therapy, Chart B is a sample reference list of Scriptures the clinician can suggest for the client to use for meditation and recitation.

A Personal Experience with Faith and Mental Health:

I recall a case earlier in my career where I was prepared to provide therapy to an African American, female teenager. The initial session was conducted with her and her mother. In the session, the mother expressed a certain level of discomfort in her daughter receiving services at the outpatient clinic, since the mother viewed the system as secular. As I remember, the mother stated that she would typically handle family problems with prayer and other faith-based methods, which did not include attending counseling. The demographics that could have naturally connected the family and I such as our shared gender and/or ethnicity were unable to overcome the mother's perception of the barrier in my ability to understand their faith-based needs, since I was unable to advertise that I was a Christian. Not necessarily having the backing from the agency or a clear treatment model on how to professionally incorporate the families identified faith into treatment, it may have been assumed by the parent that I minimally affirmed her perspective.

Given the opportunity by the family, during the course of treatment, I would have attempted to integrate their faith needs, but since the family did not return after the initial session, I did not have the opportunity to do so. The almost immediate need for some families to feel connected by their core values to the treatment model can apparently be critical.

CHAPTER 8

What is Next?

Several years ago, myself and other youth involved in an Evangelical outreach ministry were walking down the streets of Buffalo passing out Christian flyers. We placed the flyers on the windshields of many vehicles. Later that evening, I noticed that contradicting literature, such as invitations to secular events, had been placed on all of the same windshields where we had earlier distributed our Christian literature. My initial reaction was to remove the opposing literature; however, the Assistant President of the ministry directed me not to do so. She said "Let them make their own choice." Although I did not want to leave the secular information there, I now better understand her logic, which was that everyone has the right to make his or her own choice; as to what he or she will be a party to.

You have the choice of whether or not to accept what I am offering in terms of integrating faith and mental health as a potentially valid treatment option. But whether you personally agree or not, please do not harshly judge myself or others for trying to expand an area of inquiry that is worthwhile. Since the practice of religion affects a large percentage of the population, it is therefore legitimate to suggest the need for further research and funding in this area (Masters 2010, 394).

Researchers can conduct qualitative or quantitative analysis. The analysis will assess when it is feasible for clinicians working with certain populations to begin implementing faith-based interventions. For instance, should Christian clients who have matriculated through pastoral counseling start at a different point in outpatient counseling than those who did not receive pastoral counseling? Using empirical findings from these answered questions can help clinicians develop a spectrum of care, when implementing faith-based interventions. Also, from an educational standpoint, research questions will seek to determine if it would be more effective to begin introducing faith-based course material at introductory or advanced levels. Realistically, institutions of higher learning can discuss clergy co-teaching sections of the lecture regarding typical presentations of persons of faith and/or the average needs expressed in pastoral counseling.

My position is not necessarily to force a perspective of faith on anyone but rather to contribute to a growing body of work regarding the usage of biblical principles in the assessment and treatment of mental illness. You may be asking yourself if I am implying that clinicians have to be Christian to use faith-based interventions in practice. The answer is no, they do not. It helps, but it is not necessary for someone to be a Christian to make mention of Scriptures in therapy. According to some research, nonreligious therapists who used a religious form of CBT with religious clients actually had better outcomes than religious therapists using the same treatment (Masters 2010, 397). The Bible is so powerful that it will have an impact when shared; it can work as a stand-alone, so to speak.

> "For the Word that God speaks is alive and full of power
> [making it active, operative, energizing, and effective];
> it is sharper than any two-edged sword, penetrating

to the dividing line of the breath of the life (soul) and [the immortal] spirit, and of joints and marrow [of the deepest parts of our nature], exposing and sifting and analyzing and judging the very thoughts and purposes of the heart" (Heb. 4:12).

This Scripture demonstrates that even though the therapist may not believe the word of God, merely referencing biblical passages in a session can still be impactful for the client if the client believes the Scripture. In contrast, as much as I do not accept the theory of evolution, I could effectively teach that subject matter to students if I were asked to.

A Soul Sickness

As previously mentioned, sin has an undeniable impact on our souls and minds. Using the below Scripture as an example, we will further explore some possible explanations for a contaminated mind or soul in order to emphasize why the collaboration between faith and clinical practice is beneficial.

"Your eye is the lamp of your body; when your eye (your conscience) is sound and fulfilling its office, your whole body is full of light; but when it is not sound and is not fulfilling its office, your body is full of darkness. Be careful, therefore, that the light that is in you is not darkness. If then your entire body is illuminated, having no part dark, it will be wholly bright [with light], as when a lamp with its bright rays gives you light" (Luke 11:34-36).

As it relates to morality, one of the most critical aspects of the mind is the conscience. I recently spoke with an iridologist, and as she was explaining the technique she uses to assess health in the body, I was amazed. She told me that through taking pictures of the eye or iris, she could determine if there was inflammation in my body. Iridologists view the eye as a window that speaks to the overall health of the body, and likewise, from a spiritual perspective, the conscience is a window to the soul. The Bible informs us of the following:

1- The conscience is used to interpret information.
2- When the conscience is in optimal condition, the individual can properly process information.
3- There is a warning to keep the conscience healthy, because it permeates the complete individual.
4- When not functioning properly, a seared conscience can lead to the development of mental health issues and, ultimately, deviant behavior.
5- Obedience to The Gospel of Christ is what can heal the conscience.

"Consciences that are seared (cauterized)" (1 Tim. 4:2, author's paraphrase), in many cases, can lead to maladaptive and destructive behaviors. This occurs mainly because the conscience serves as an internal guide to help individuals inherently know the difference between right and wrong. When this moral compass is broken, there is no longer an internal path to help us navigate through good and evil. A continual lack of ability to discern what is right and wrong propels us to do whatever we want without a sense of remorse or conviction. A broken moral compass is a potential cause for criminal behavior without remorse or empathy. The rehabilitation of the conscience is a function of the Gospel of Christ.

The Collaboration between the
Church and Clinical Practice

Thus far, I have addressed the need for professionals to use faith in practice, but there is also a need for collaboration between clergy and practitioners to produce a working referral system. As reported in a study, many clergy members actually feel ill-equipped to address the mental health needs of the parishioners they interact with (Masters 2010, 558). This is particularly alarming because people with diagnosable mental illnesses often turn to their trusted clergy members prior to a mental health professional. Team-work that allows for referrals between clergy and health-care professionals is actually supported by the Bible, as Jesus said "…sick people need the doctor, not the healthy ones", but "I came to save the lost" (Mark 2:17; Luke 19:10, author's paraphrase). With the increase in manifestations of psychological and mental illnesses in congregations, clergy can actually benefit from additional training in clinical assessment. The important distinction in the nature of these referrals is that God saves or heals the soul through faith in Christ while medical doctors focus more on healing the body through their medicinal interventions.

Potential Drawbacks of Collaboration
between Faith and Practice

Since we have discussed the advantages of incorporating faith into mental health training, I will give a small voice to a suggested disadvantage. Some have argued that using religion in therapy can place more emphasis on this construct than is necessary (Masters 2010, 395). In other words, some clinicians might be of the opinion that discussing

God in therapy is a distraction because it would distract from the real nature of the client's mental health issue. Not surprisingly, however, I disagree with this perspective. The concept of "meeting the client where he or she is" is also appropriate for matters of faith. Majority of mentally ill persons and their families who believed in supernatural causes resorted to faith healing; before turning to psychiatry (Kar 2008, 738). Based on these results one could suggest if faith is not taken seriously in treatment, there will remain a certain percentage of people who will not seek professional help, if their practice of faith will remain insignificant.

Given this feedback, clinicians and educators need to seriously consider the perspective of the client and include their faith in the healing process, when faith is a factor. This should be done in a true spirit of support, as recent reports indicate a desire for religious values to not only be respected but also to be actively incorporated into therapeutic practice (Masters 2010, 394-395).

A Personal Experience with
Faith and Mental Health:

In 2013, I took a mini vacation to Virginia Beach. During that time, I met healthcare professionals who were also professors and actively involved in their churches. We discussed what potential next steps were needed in closing the gaps between church representatives and mental health practitioners. Ultimately, we practitioners agreed that a future goal would be to provide comprehensive services to parishioners from a faith-based orientation. I was pleased to know that these goals are actively being pursued in other areas of the country.

As a Christian and mental health provider, the goal of this integration becomes personal. I have felt poorly discussing my life with mental health practitioners who were uninformed and unopened to my perspective, so I want to attempt to prevent other Christian clients from experiencing this type of perceived rejection.

Epilogue

This book is entitled "The Spirit of a Sound Mind," derived from the following Bible quote: "...[He has given us a spirit] of power and of love and of a calm *and* well-balanced mind *and* discipline *and* self-control" (2 Tim. 1:7, author's paraphrase). A sound mind is sensible, balanced and disciplined. Many people are struggling emotionally and psychologically because they have not developed the type of mind that God intended for them.

Obtaining a sound mind is the goal of any therapy regardless of the modality, such as family and marriage counseling, individual or group therapy. Helping a client gain a sense of control over his or her life is an expectation of each professional helper, whether clinical psychologist, social worker or licensed mental health counselor. A successful discharge from therapy is contingent upon the impartation of knowledge and tools that provide the basis for continued discipline on behalf of the client.

Currently, the education curriculums of many institutions of higher learning are out of balance because there is not adequate representation regarding the needs people of faith will have in clinical settings. Bringing balance to the systems that impact society is equally as important as balance is to the individual. Preparing future clinicians or enhancing the knowledge of current clinicians on how to effectively engage with people of faith in clinical settings will help bring equilibrium to needs and abilities.

With increasing social pressures and expectations, individuals and families are struggling to maintain a sense of balance now more than ever. Clients are more likely to experience a successful recovery when offered treatment from a holistic approach that acknowledges and embraces faith-based opportunities that promote healing. It is my hope that all clients will develop a sound mind.

Hopefully, as a result of reading this book, you now have a desire to know more about the God of the Bible and even have a personal relationship with Him. No matter who you are, whether you are a student, a professional or neither, you have or will have battles and problems that will impact your mind. Please, do not think that only "crazy" people experience psychological distress. It is true that not everyone will experience hallucinations or become dangerously delusional, but you may suffer from extreme anxiety and fear that keeps you on edge, or you could become acquainted with debilitating sadness. It is important to know that you are not alone; other people have and will experience similar mental afflictions. You may be thinking "is it possible for someone else to have these same problems? I don't believe it." Please know that you are not alone. I would like to share the opportunity of salvation with you, as the Bible states:

> "because if you acknowledge and confess with your lips
> that Jesus is Lord and in your heart believe (adhere to,
> trust in, and rely on the truth) that God raised Him
> from the dead, you will be saved" (Rom. 10:9).

The process for salvation is believing and confessing that Jesus is Lord and placing our trust in Him alone. No matter how "good" we might feel that we are, our own good works or deeds are unacceptable to God for the pardon of our sins. This is why we need God's chosen Savior, Jesus Christ, "For we have all become like one who is unclean [ceremonially, like a leper], and all our righteousness (our best deeds of rightness and justice) is like filthy rags or a polluted garment; we all fade like a leaf, and our iniquities, like the wind, take us away [far from God's favor, hurrying us toward destruction]" (Isa. 64:6).

You may not have come from a home environment where the Gospel was shared, or your family may not have believed in God, or still yet, you may have served God at one time but strayed away from practicing your faith, but whatever your history, your future awaits you. You can accept Jesus Christ right now and begin a path to lasting peace. If you have accepted Christ, the Bible states that your name is now written in what is referred to as the Lamb's book of Life, where "God has written a record of the names of those who have lived for Him on earth" (Rev. 21:27, author's paraphrase).

If you have not accepted Christ into your life and would like to do so, I ask you to pray this prayer: I acknowledge that I am a sinner and repent of all my sins and ask for Your forgiveness. I believe in the Gospel of Jesus Christ; that He is God's Son, was born of a virgin, died on the cross for my sins, was buried, rose from the grave and will return to gather His children. I confess that Jesus is Lord. I ask You fill me with Your Holy Spirit, in Jesus' name, Amen.

If you prayed that prayer and genuinely meant it, you are now a Christian! It is that simple. It is imperative now that you locate a Bible-based church and join. If you cannot access a church for one reason or another, you may be able to view Christian programming on television or on the internet (see website in foreword). Just remember, any doctrine you endorse must be examined against Scripture.

It is my sincere hope that as a result of reading this book you have not only been exposed to an additional lens through which to view and treat mental illness, but that you will become an advocate of this approach as well.

Contact and Booking Information

Please contact Shatina C. Barr at Cheree's Consulting, P.O. Box 333, Lackawanna, New York 14218 if you are interested in requesting seminars regarding this book, or have accepted salvation or would like to receive other mental health material produced by this company. Ms. Barr is also an ordained minister of the Gospel and travels to spread the good news of Jesus Christ. Please visit her website at www.chereesconsulting.com or contact her by phone at (716) 812-0472.

Products by the author

Inspirational apparel
CD's-Sermon

References

Carlos, M., Del Rio, and Lyle J. White. "Separating Spirituality From Religiosity: A Hylomorphic Attitudinal Perspective." *Psychology of Religion and Spirituality* 4, no. 2 (2012): 123-42. Accessed November 13, 2012. DOI: 10.1037/a0027552.

Dein, Simon, Christopher C.H. Cook, Andrew Powell, and Sarah Eagger. "Special Article." *The Psychiatrist Formerly the Psychiatric Bulletin Religion, Spirituality and Mental Health*, no. 34 (2010): 63-64, Accessed November 13, 2012. DOI: 10.1192/pb.bp.109.025924. http://pb.rcpsych.org/content/34/2/63.full.

Innocence Blog. "No Apology, But 54 Million from City of Peekskill to Exoneree." (blog), September 5, 2013 (4:00p.m.) Accessed September 14, 2013.
http://www.innonceproject.org/Content/
No_Apology_But_54_
Million_from_City_of_Peekskill_to_Exoneree.php

Jobe, Martin. *The Evolution of Creationist: A Laymen's Guide to the Conflict between the Bible and Evolutionary Theory*. Rockwall, Texas: Biblical Discipleship Publishers, 2002. 13, 67.

kar, Nilamadhab. "Resort to faith-healing practices in the pathway to care for mental illness: a study on psychiatric inpatients in Orissa." *Mental Health, Religion & Culture* 11, n 7 (2008): 729-740. Accessed November 13, 2012. DOI: 10.1080/13674670802018950.

Leavey, Gerard, Kate Loewenthal, and Michael King. "Challenges to Sanctuary: The Clergy as a Resource for Mental Health Care in the Community." *Social Science & Medicine*, no. 65 (2007): 548-59, Accessed November 13, 2012. DOI: 10.1016/j. socscimed.2007.03.050.

Masters, Kevin S. "The Role of Religion in Therapy: Time for Psychologists to Have a Little Faith?" *Cognitive and Behavioral Practice* 17 (2010) 393-400. Accessed November 13, 2012. DOI: 10.1016/j.cbpra.2009.11.003.

Made in United States
North Haven, CT
20 April 2023

35675255R00069